Krishnamurti to Himself

R. L. Brower

Ph (403) 439-1569

Krishnamurti to Himself

— His Last Journal —

J. KRISHNAMURTI

HarperSanFrancisco

A Division of HarperCollins*Publishers*

FIRST HARPERCOLLINS PAPERBACK EDITION PUBLISHED IN 1993

Library of Congress Cataloging-in-Publication Data

Krishnamurti, J. (Jiddu), 1895–
    Krishnamurti to himself : his last journal / J. Krishnamurti. —
1st HarperCollins pbk. ed.
      p. cm.
    ISBN 0-06-250649-8
    I. Title.
B5134.K753K754   1993
181' .4—dc20
[B]   92-53255
                                             CIP

---

97   RRD(H)   10 9 8 7 6 5 4

FOREWORD

THIS BOOK IS unique in that it is the only one of Krishnamurti's publications which records words spoken into a tape-recorder while he was quite alone.

After the success of *Krishnamurti's Journal*, published in 1982, he was urged to continue it but, since by then his hand had become rather shaky (he was eighty-seven), it was suggested that instead of writing it, which would tire him, he should dictate it to himself. This idea appealed to him. However, he could not start at once because he was on the point of flying to India where he would have no time to himself. On his return to California, in February 1983, he dictated the first of the pieces contained in this volume into a new Sony tape-recorder.

All the dictations except one were recorded from his home, Pine Cottage, in the Ojai Valley, some eighty miles north of Los Angeles. He would dictate in the mornings, while in bed after breakfast, undisturbed.

Krishnamurti had first stayed at Pine Cottage with his brother in 1922, when it was lent to him by a friend, and it was there, in August, '22, that he underwent a spiritual experience that transformed his life. Soon afterwards, a Trust was formed to which money was subscribed to buy the cottage and six acres of surrounding land. In 1978 a beautiful new house was built incorporating the cottage in which Krishnamurti retained his original bedroom and a small sitting-room.

His dictations were not as finished as his writings, and at times his voice would wander away from the recorder to become rather distant, so, unlike his *Notebook* and *Journal*, some slight editing has been necessary for the sake of clarity.

5

The reader gets very close to Krishnamurti in these pieces — almost, it seems at moments, into his very consciousness. In a few of them he introduces an imaginary visitor who comes to question him and draw him out.

The gist of Krishnamurti's teaching is here, and the descriptions of nature with which he begins most of the pieces may for many, who regard him as a poet as well as a philosopher, quieten their whole being so that they become intuitively receptive to what follows. There are repetitions, but these seem somehow necessary in order to emphasize his meaning, and they clearly show how every day was a completely new day to him, free from all burdens of the past.

Strangely, the last piece, and perhaps the most beautiful, is about death. It is the last occasion on which we shall ever hear Krishnamurti discoursing to himself. Two years later he died in this same bedroom at Pine Cottage.

M.L.

Krishnamurti to Himself

THERE IS A tree by the river and we have been watching it day after day for several weeks when the sun is about to rise. As the sun rises slowly over the horizon, over the trees, this particular tree becomes all of a sudden golden. All the leaves are bright with life and as you watch it as the hours pass by, that tree whose name does not matter — what matters is that beautiful tree — an extraordinary quality seems to spread all over the land, over the river. And as the sun rises a little higher the leaves begin to flutter, to dance. And each hour seems to give to that tree a different quality. Before the sun rises it has a sombre feeling, quiet, far away, full of dignity. And as the day begins, the leaves with the light on them dance and give it that peculiar feeling that one has of great beauty. By midday its shadow has deepened and you can sit there protected from the sun, never feeling lonely, with the tree as your companion. As you sit there, there is a relationship of deep abiding security and a freedom that only trees can know.

Towards the evening when the western skies are lit up by the setting sun, the tree gradually becomes sombre, dark, closing in on itself. The sky has become red, yellow, green, but the tree remains quiet, hidden, and is resting for the night.

If you establish a relationship with it then you have relationship with mankind. You are responsible then for that tree and for the trees of the world. But if you have no relationship with the living things on this earth you may lose whatever relationship you have with humanity, with human beings. We never look deeply into the quality of a tree; we never really touch it, feel its solidity, its rough bark, and hear the sound that is part of the tree. Not the sound of wind through the leaves, not the breeze of a morning that flutters the leaves, but its own sound, the sound of the trunk and the silent sound of the roots. You must be extraordinarily sensitive to hear the sound. This sound is not the noise of the world, not the noise of the chattering of the mind, not the vulgarity of human quarrels and human warfare but sound as part of the universe.

It is odd that we have so little relationship with nature, with the insects and the leaping frog and the owl that hoots among the hills calling for its mate. We never seem to have a feeling for all living things on the earth. If we could establish a deep abiding relationship with nature we would never kill an animal for our appetite, we would never harm, vivisect, a monkey, a dog, a guinea pig for our benefit. We would find other ways to heal our wounds, heal our bodies. But the healing of the mind is something totally different. That healing gradually takes place if you are with nature, with that orange on the tree, and the blade of grass that pushes through the cement, and the hills covered, hidden, by the clouds.

This is not sentiment or romantic imagination but a reality of a relationship with everything that lives and moves on the earth. Man has killed millions of whales and is still killing them. All that we derive from their slaughter can be had through other means. But apparently man loves to kill things, the fleeting deer, the marvellous gazelle and the great elephant. We love to kill each other. This killing of other human beings has never stopped throughout the history of man's life on this earth. If we could, and we must, establish a deep long abiding relationship with nature, with the actual trees, the bushes, the flowers, the grass and the fast moving clouds, then we would never slaughter another human being for any reason whatsoever. Organized murder is war, and though we demonstrate against a particular war, the nuclear, or any other kind of war, we have never demonstrated against war. We have never said that to kill another human being is the greatest sin on earth.

FLYING AT 41,000 feet from one continent to another you see nothing but snow, miles of snow; all the mountains and the hills are covered with snow, and the rivers too are frozen. You see them wandering, meandering, all over the land. And far below, the distant farms are covered with ice and snow. It is a long, tiresome flight of eleven hours. The passengers were chattering away. There was a couple behind one and they never stopped talking, never looked at the glory of those marvellous hills and mountains, never looked at the other passengers. Apparently they were absorbed in their own thoughts, in their own problems, in their chatterings. And at last, after a tedious, calm flight, in the dead of winter, you land at the town on the Pacific.

After the noise and the bustle, you leave that ugly, sprawling, vulgar, shouting city and the endless shops selling almost all the same things. You leave all that behind as you go round the coast highway of the blue Pacific, following the seashore, on a beautiful road, wandering through the hills, meeting the sea often; and as you leave the Pacific behind and enter into the country, winding over various small hills, peaceful, quiet, full of that strange dignity of the country, you enter the valley. You have been there for the last sixty years, and each time you are astonished to enter into this valley. It is quiet, almost untouched by man. You enter into this valley which is almost like a vast cup, a nest. Then you leave the little village and climb to about 1,400 feet, passing rows and rows of orange orchards and groves. The air is perfumed with orange blossom. The whole valley is filled with that scent. And the smell of it is in your mind, in your heart, in your whole body. It is the most extraordinary feeling of living in a perfume that will last for about three weeks or more. And there is a quietness in the mountains, a dignity. And each time you

11

look at those hills and the high mountain, which is over 6,000 feet, you are really surprised that such a country exists. Each time you come to this quiet, peaceful valley there is a feeling of strange aloofness, of deep silence and the vast spreading of slow time.

Man is trying to spoil the valley but it has been preserved. And the mountains that morning were extraordinarily beautiful. You could almost touch them. The majesty, the vast sense of permanency is there in them. And you enter quietly into the house where you have lived for over sixty years and the atmosphere, the air, is, if one can use that word, holy; you can feel it. You can almost touch it. As it has rained considerably, for it is the rainy season, all the hills and the little folds of the mountain are green, flourishing, full—the earth is smiling with such delight, with some deep quiet understanding of its own existence.

'You have said over and over again that the mind, or if you prefer it, the brain, must be quiet, must empty itself of all the knowledge it has gathered, not only to be free but to comprehend something that is not of time or thought or of any action. You have said this in different ways in most of your talks and I find this awfully difficult, not only to grasp the idea, the depth of it but the feeling of quiet emptiness, if I can use that word. I never could feel my way into it. I have tried various methods to end the chattering of the mind, the endless occupation with something or other, this very occupation creating its problems. And as one lives one is caught up in all this. This is our daily life, the tedium, the talk that goes on in a family, and if there isn't talking there is always the television or a book. The mind seems to demand that it should be occupied, that it should move from one thing to another, from knowledge to knowledge, from action to action with the everlasting movement of thought.'

'As we pointed out, thought cannot be stopped by determination, by a decision of the will, or the urgent pressing desire to enter into that quality of quiet, still emptiness.'

12

'I find myself envious for something which I think, which I feel, to be true, which I would like to have, but it has always eluded me, it has always gone beyond my grasp. I have come, as I have often come, to talk with you: why in my daily life, in my business life, is there not the stability, the endurance of that quietness? Why isn't this in my life? I have asked myself what am I to do. I also realize I cannot do much, or I can't do anything at all about it. But it is there nagging. I can't leave it alone. If only I could experience it once, then that very memory will nourish me, then that very remembrance will give a significance to a really rather silly life. So I have come to enquire, to probe into this matter: why does the mind — perhaps the word brain may be better — demand that it should be occupied?'

THE OTHER DAY as one was walking along a secluded wooded lane far from the noise and the brutality and the vulgarity of civilization, right away from everything that was put together by man, there was a sense of great quietness, enveloping all things — serene, distant and full of the sound of the earth. As you walked along quietly, not disturbing the things of the earth around you, the bushes, the trees, the crickets and the birds, suddenly round a bend there were two small creatures quarrelling with each other, fighting in their small way. One was trying to drive off the other. The other was intruding, trying to get into the other's little hole, and the owner was fighting it off. Presently the owner won and the other ran off. Again there was quietness, a sense of deep solitude. And as you looked up, the path climbed high into the mountains, the waterfall was gently murmuring down the side of the path; there was great beauty and infinite dignity, not the dignity achieved by man that seems so vain and arrogant. The little creature had identified itself with its home, as we human beings do. We are always trying to identify ourselves with our race, with our culture, with those things which we believe in, with some mystical figure, or some saviour, some kind of super authority. Identifying with something seems to be the nature of man. Probably we have derived this feeling from that little animal.

One wonders why this craving, longing, for identification exists. One can understand the identification with one's physical needs — the necessary things, clothes, food, shelter and so on. But inwardly, inside the skin as it were, we try to identify ourselves with the past, with tradition, with some fanciful

14

romantic image, a symbol much cherished. And surely in this identification there is a sense of security, safety, a sense of being owned and of possessing. This gives great comfort. One takes comfort, security, in any form of illusion. And man apparently needs many illusions.

In the distance there is the hoot of an owl and there is a deep-throated reply from the other side of the valley. It is still dawn. The noise of the day has not begun and everything is quiet. There is something strange and holy where the sun arises. There is a prayer, a chant to the dawn, to that strange quiet light. That early morning, the light was subdued, there was no breeze and all the vegetation, the trees, the bushes, were quiet, still, waiting. Waiting for the sun to arise. And perhaps the sun would not come up for another half hour or so, and the dawn was slowly covering the earth with a strange stillness.

Gradually, slowly, the topmost mountain was getting brighter and the sun was touching it, golden, clear, and the snow was pure, untouched by the light of day.

As you climbed, leaving the little village paths down below, the noise of the earth, the crickets, the quails and other birds began their morning song, their chant, their rich worship of the day. And as the sun arose you were part of that light and had left behind everything that thought had put together. You completely forgot yourself. The psyche was empty of its struggles and its pains. And as you walked, climbed, there was no sense of separateness, no sense of being even a human being.

The morning mist was gathering slowly in the valley, and that mist was you, getting more and more thick, more and more into the fancy, the romance, the idiocy of one's own life. And after a long period of time you came down. There was the murmur of the wind, insects, the calls of many birds. And as you came down the mist was disappearing. There were streets, shops, and the glory of the dawn was fast fading away. And you began your daily

15

routine, caught in the habit of work, the contentions between man and man, the divisions of identification, the division of ideologies, the preparations for wars, your own inward pain and the everlasting sorrow of man.

IT WAS A cool fresh morning and there was the light that California alone has, especially the southern part of it. It is really quite an extraordinary light.

We have travelled probably all over the world, most of the world at least, have seen various lights and clouds in many parts of the earth. The clouds in Holland are very close; here in California the clouds against the blue sky seem to hold the light everlastingly — the light that great clouds have, with their extraordinary shape and quality.

It was a cool, very nice morning. And as you climbed the rocky path up to the great height and looked down into the valley and saw the row upon row of orange trees, avocados and the hills that surround the valley, it was as though you were out of this world, so completely lost were you to all things, to the weariness, to man's ugly reactions and actions. You left all that behind as you climbed up and up the very rocky path. You left behind far below you the vanity, the arrogance, the vulgarity of uniforms, decorations spread all over your chest, and the vanity and strange costumes of priests. You left all that behind.

And as you went up you nearly trod on a mother with her dozen or more little baby quails and they scattered with chirping into the bushes. As you went on up and looked back, the mother had again gathered them round her and they were all quite secure under the wings of their mother.

You had to climb hour after hour to reach the great height. Some days you saw a bear a little way off and it paid no attention. And the deer across the gulley, they too seemed unconcerned. At last you reached the height of a rocky plateau, and across the hills to the south-west you saw the distant sea, so blue, so quiet, so infinitely far away. You sat on a rock, smooth, cracked, where the sun must for century upon century, without any regret, have cracked it. And in the little cracks you saw tiny little living things scurrying about, and there was that utter silence, complete and infinite. A very large bird — they call it a condor — was circling in the sky. Apart from that movement there was nothing astir except these tiny little insects. but there was that silence that exists only where man has not been before; it was so peaceful.

You left everything behind in that little village so far below you. Literally everything: your identity, if you had any, your belongings, the possession of your experiences, your memories of things that had meant something to you — you left all that behind, down below there amidst the shining groves and orchards. Here there was absolute silence and you were totally alone.

It was a marvellous morning and the cool air which was becoming colder wrapped round you, and you were completely lost to everything. There was nothing and beyond nothing.

You should really forget the word meditation. That word has been corrupted. The ordinary meaning of that word — to ponder over, to consider, to think about — is rather trivial and ordinary. If you want to understand the nature of meditation you should really forget the word because you cannot possibly measure with words that which is not measurable, that which is beyond all measure. No words can convey it, nor any systems, modes of thought, practice or discipline. Meditation — or rather if we could find another word which has not been so mutilated, made so ordinary, corrupt, which has become the means of earning a great deal of money — if you can put aside the word, then you begin quietly and gently to feel a movement that is not of time. Again, the word movement implies time — what is meant is a movement that has no beginning or end. A movement in the sense of a wave: wave upon wave, starting from nowhere and with no beach to crash upon. It is an endless wave.

Time, however slow it is, is rather tiresome. Time means

growth, evolution, to become, to achieve, to learn, to change. And time is not the way of that which lies far beyond the word meditation. Time has nothing to do with it. Time is the action of will, of desire, and desire cannot in any way [word or words inaudible here] — it lies far beyond the word meditation.

Here, sitting on that rock, with the blue sky — it is astonishingly blue — the air is so pure, unpolluted. Far beyond this range is the desert. You can see it, miles of it. It is really a timeless perception of that which is. It is only that perception which can say it is.

You sat there watching for what seemed many days, many years, many centuries. As the sun was going down to the sea you made your way down to the valley and everything around you was alight, that blade of grass, that sumac [a wild bush], the towering eucalyptus and the flowering earth. It took time to come down as it had taken time to go up. But that which has no time cannot be measured by words. And meditation is only a word. The roots of heaven are in deep abiding silence.

IT WAS REALLY a most lovely clear beautiful morning. There was dew on every leaf. And as the sun rose slowly, quietly spreading over the beautiful land, there was great peace in this valley. The trees were full of oranges, small ones but many. Gradually the sun lit every tree and every orange. When you sat on that veranda overlooking the valley, there were the long shadows of the morning. The shadow is as beautiful as the tree. We wanted to go out, not in a car, but out among the trees, smell the fresh air and the scent of many oranges and the flowers, and hear the sound of the earth.

Later on one climbed right to the very top of the hill, overlooking the wide valley. The earth doesn't belong to anyone. It is the land upon which all of us are to live for many years, ploughing, reaping and destroying.

You are always a guest on this earth and have the austerity of a guest. Austerity is far deeper than owning only a few things. The very word austerity has been spoilt by the monks, by the sannyasis, by the hermits. Sitting on that high hill alone in the solitude of many things, many rocks and little animals and ants, that word had no meaning.

Over the hills in the far distance was the wide, shining, sparkling sea. We have broken up the earth as yours and mine — your nation, my nation, your flag and his flag, this particular religion and the religion of the distant man. The world, the earth, is divided, broken up. And for it we fight and wrangle, and the politicians exult in their power to maintain this division, never looking at the world as a whole. They haven't got the global mind. They never feel nor ever perceive the immense possibility of having no nationality, no division, they can never perceive the ugliness of their power, their position and their sense of importance. They are like you or another, only they occupy the seat of power with their petty little desires and ambitions, and so maintain apparently, as long as man has been on this earth, the tribal attitude towards life. They don't have a mind that is not committed to any issue, to any ideals, ideologies — a mind that steps beyond the division of race, culture, and the religions man has invented.

Governments must exist as long as man is not a light to himself, as long as he does not live his daily life with order, care, diligently working, watching, learning. He would rather be told what to do. He has been told what to do by the ancients, by the priests, by the gurus, and he accepts their orders, their peculiar destructive disciplines as though they were gods on this earth, as though they knew all the implications of this extraordinarily complex life.

Sitting there, high above all the trees, on a rock that has its own sound like every living thing on this earth, and watching the blue sky, clear, spotless, one wonders how long it will take for man to learn to live on this earth without wrangles, rows, wars and conflict. Man has created the conflict by his division of the earth, linguistically, culturally, superficially. One wonders how long man, who has evolved through so many centuries of pain and grief, anxiety and pleasure, fear and conflict, will take to live a different way of life.

As you sat quietly without movement, a bob cat, a lynx, came down. As the wind was blowing up the valley it was not aware of the smell of that human being. It was purring, rubbing itself against a rock, its small tail up, and enjoying the marvel of the earth. Then it disappeared down the hill among the bushes. It was protecting its lair, its cave or its sleeping place. It was protecting what it needs, protecting its own kittens, and watching for danger. It was afraid of man more than anything else, man who believes in god, man who prays, the man of wealth with his gun, with his casual killing. You could almost smell that bob cat as it passed by you. You were so motionless, so utterly still that it

21

never even looked at you; you were part of that rock, part of the environment.

Why, one wonders, does man not realize that one can live peacefully, without wars, without violence; how long will it take him, how many centuries upon centuries to realize this? From the past centuries of a thousand yesterdays, he has not learned. What he is now will be his future.

It was getting too hot on that rock. You could feel the gathering heat through your trousers so you got up and went down and followed the lynx which had long since disappeared. There were other creatures: the gopher, the king snake, and a rattler [rattle-snake]. They were silently going about their business. The morning air disappeared; gradually the sun was in the west. It would take an hour or two before it set behind those hills with the marvellous shape of the rock and the evening colours of blue and red and yellow. Then the night would begin, the night sounds would fill the air; only late in the night would there be utter silence. The roots of heaven are of great emptiness, for in emptiness there is energy, incalculable, vast and profound.

THIS END OF the valley, particularly on this lovely quiet morning, was peaceful, there was no sound of traffic. The hills were behind you and the tallest mountain in this region was over 6,000 feet. This house is surrounded by orchards, bright yellow oranges, and the sky was blue without a single cloud. You could hear the murmur of bees among the flowers in the still quiet morning. The old oak tree* behind the house was a great age; the strong winds had broken many dead branches. It has survived many storms, many summers of great heat and the cold winters. Probably it could tell you a lot of stories but this morning it was very quiet, there was no breeze. Everything around you was full of green and bright oranges, yellow and shining, and perfume filled the air — the perfume of jasmine.

This valley is far from all the noise and the bustle of human traffic, of humanity, of all the ugly things that are going on in the world. The orange trees were just beginning to show their fresh young flowers. The scent of it would fill the valley in a week or two and there would be the hum of thousands of bees. It was a peaceful morning and beyond all this lay the sick world, a world that is becoming more and more dangerous, more and more corrupt, vastly dull in search of entertainment, religious and otherwise. The superficiality of existence is thriving. Money seems to be the greatest value in life, and with it naturally goes power, position and the sorrow of it all.

'On such a beautiful morning I want to talk over with you a rather sad subject, frightening, the sense of apprehension that pervades humanity and myself. I would really like to understand,

*The Californian evergreen holm oak.

23

not merely intellectually or descriptively, why, with so many others, I dread the ending of life.

'We kill so easily — it is called blood sport, shooting birds for amusement to show off one's skill, chasing the fox, killing by the million the things of the sea; death seems to be everywhere. Sitting on this quiet veranda, looking at those bright yellow oranges, it is difficult — or rather it seems so unseemly — to talk over something that is so frightening. Man throughout all the ages has never really solved or understood the thing called death.

'Naturally I have studied various religious and scientific rationalizations, beliefs, and they assume realities; some of them are logical, comforting, but the fact remains that there is always the fear of the unknown.

'I was discussing this fact with a friend of mine whose wife has recently died. He was a rather lonely man and he was inclined not only to live in his memories but also to find out for himself through seances, mediums and all that whether his wife, whom he really loved, had just evaporated into thin air, or was there still a continuity of her in another dimension, in another world than this?

'He said, "Strangely enough I found that at one of these seances the medium mentioned my name and said that she had a message from my wife. And the message was something only known to her and me. Of course the medium may have read my thoughts or my wife may exist. That thought was in the air, the thought of that secret which was between us. I have asked many people of their experiences. It all seems so vain and rather stupid, including the message from my wife which was so trivial, so deeply meaningless." I don't want to discuss with you whether there is an entity of a person which continues after death. That is not my interest. Some say there is a continuity, others say there is total annihilation. This contradiction — annihilation, total ending of a person or the continuity of that individual — has been in all literature, from the ancients to the present day. But to me, all this is beside the point. Its validity is still in the realm of speculation, superstition, belief and the desire for comfort, hope. I am really not concerned with all that. I really mean this. I am at least quite certain of that. But I would like to have a dialogue with you, if I may, about what is the meaning of it all — this whole business of living and dying. Is it all utterly meaningless, vague, without any depth, without any significance whatsoever? Millions have died and millions will be born and continue and die. I am one of those. I always ask myself: what is the meaning of living and dying? The earth is beautiful, I have travelled a great deal, talked to many people who are supposed to be wise and learned, but they too die.

'I have come a long way so perhaps you would be good enough to take time and have the quiet patience to talk over this subject with me.'

'Doubt is a precious thing. It cleanses, purifies the mind. The very questioning, the very fact that the seed of doubt is in one, helps to clarify our investigation. Not only doubting what all the others have said, including the whole concept of regeneration, and the Christian belief and dogma of resurrection, but also the Asiatic world's acceptance that there is continuity. In doubting, questioning all that, there is a certain freedom which is necessary for our enquiry. If one can put all that aside, actually, not merely verbally but negate all that deep within oneself, then one has no illusion. And it is necessary to be totally free from any kind of illusion — the illusions that are imposed upon us and the illusions that we create for ourselves. All illusions are the things that we play with, and if one is serious then they have no place whatsoever, nor does faith come into all this.

'So having set aside all that, not for the moment but seeing the falseness of all that, the mind is not caught in the falsehood that man has invented about death, about god, about all the rituals that thought has created. There must be freedom of opinion and judgement, for then only can one deliberately, actually, hesitantly explore into the meaning of daily living and dying —

25

existence and the end of existence. If one is prepared for this, or if one is willing, or even better if one is actually, deeply concerned to find out the truth of the matter (living and dying is a very complex problem, an issue that requires a very careful examination) where should we begin? With life or with death? With living or with the ending of that which we call living?'

'I am over fifty, and have lived rather extravagantly, keeping an interest in many, many things. I think I would like to begin — I am rather hesitant, I am rather doubtful where I should begin.'

'I think we ought to begin with the beginning of existence, man's existence, with one's existence as a human being.'

'I was born into a fairly well-to-do family, carefully educated and brought up. I have been in several businesses and I have sufficient money; I am a single man now. I have been married, had two children, who all died in a car accident. And I have never married again. I think I should like to begin with my childhood. From the beginning, like every other child in the world, poor or rich, there was a well developed psyche, the self-centred activity. It is strange, as you look back upon it, that it begins from very early childhood, that possessive continuity of me as J. Smith. He went through school, expanding, aggressive, arrogant, bored, then into college and university. And as my father was in a good business I went into his Company. I reached the top, and on the death of my wife and children, I began this enquiry. As happens to all human beings, it was a shock, a pain — the loss of the three, the memories associated with them. And when the shock of it was over I began to enquire, to read, to ask, to travel in different parts of the world, talking the matter over with some of the so-called spiritual leaders, the gurus. I read a great deal but I was never satisfied. So I think we ought to begin, if I may suggest, with the actual living — the daily building up of my cultivated, circumscribed mind. And I am that. You see, my life has been that. My life is nothing exceptional. Probably I would be considered upper middle class, and for a time it was pleasurable, exciting, and at other times dull, weary, and monotonous. But the death of my wife and children somehow pulled me out of that. I haven't become morbid but I want to know the truth of it all, if there is such a thing as truth about living and dying.'

'How is the psyche, the ego, the self, the I, the person, put together? How has this thing come into being, from which arises the concept of the individual, the "me", separate from all others? How is this momentum set going — this momentum, this sense of the I, the self? We will use the word "self" to include the person, the name, the form, the characteristics, the ego. How is this self born? Does the self come into being with certain characteristics transmitted from the parents? Is the self merely a series of reactions? Is the self merely the continuity of centuries of tradition? Is the self put together by circumstances, through accidents, happenings? Is the self the result of evolution — evolution being the gradual process of time, emphasizing, giving importance to the self? Or, as some maintain, especially the religious world, does the outward shell of the self really contain within itself the soul and the ancient concept of the Hindus, of the Buddhists? Does the self come into being through the society which man has created, which gives strength to the formula that you are separate from the rest of humanity? All these have certain truths in them, certain facts, and all these constitute the self. And the self has been given tremendous importance in this world. The expression of the self in the democratic world is called freedom, and in the totalitarian world, that freedom is suppressed, denied and punished. So would you say that instinct begins in the child with the urge to possess? This also exists in the animals, so perhaps we have derived from the animals this instinct to possess. Where there is any kind of possession there must be the beginning of the self. And from this instinct, this reaction, the self gradually increases in strength, in vitality, and

27

becomes well-established. The possession of a house, the possession of land, the possession of knowledge, the possession of certain capacities — all this is the movement of the self. And this movement gives the feeling of separateness as the individual.

'Now you can go much further into details: is the you, the self, separate from the rest of mankind? Are you, because you have a separate name, a separate physical organism, certain tendencies different from another's, perhaps a talent — does that make you an individual? This idea that each one of us throughout the world is separate from another, is that an actuality? Or may the whole concept be illustory just as we have divided the world into separate communities, nations, which is really a glorified form of tribalism? This concern with oneself and the community being different from other communities, other selves — is that in actuality real? Of course you may say it is real because you are an American, and others are French, Russian, Indian, Chinese and so on. This linguistic, cultural, religious difference has brought about havoc in the world — terrible wars, incalculable harm. And also, of course, in certain aspects there is great beauty in it, in the expression of certain talents, as a painter, as a musician, as a scientist and so on. Would you consider yourself as a separate individual with a separate brain which is yours and nobody else's? It is your thinking, and your thinking is supposedly different from another's. But is thinking individual at all? Or is there only thinking, which is shared by all humanity, whether you are the most scientifically talented person or the most ignorant, primitive?

'All these questions and more arise when we are considering the death of a human being. So would you, looking at all this — the reactions, the name, the form, the possessiveness, the impulse to be separate from another, sustained by society and by religion — would you in examining all this logically, sanely, reasonably, consider yourself to be an individual? This is an important question in the context of the meaning of death.'

'I see what you are driving at. I have an intuitive comprehension, cognizance, that as long as I think that I am an individual, my thinking is separate from the thinking of others — my anxiety, my sorrow is separate from the rest of humanity. I have a feeling — please correct me — that I have reduced a vast complex living of the rest of mankind to a very small, petty little affair. Are you saying in effect that I am not an individual at all? My thinking is not mine? And my brain is not mine, separate from others? Is this what you are hinting at? Is this what you are maintaining? Is this your conclusion?'

'If one may point out, the word "conclusion" isn't justified. To conclude means to shut down, to end — conclude an argument, conclude a peace after a war. We are not concluding anything; we are just pointing out, because we must move away from conclusions, from finality and so on. Such an assertion limits, brings a narrowness into our enquiry. But the *fact*, the observable rational fact, is that your thinking and the thinking of another are similar. The expression of your thinking may vary; you may express something in one way if you are an artist, and another person, who is not an artist, may express it in another way. You judge, evaluate, according to the expression, and the expression then divides you into an artist and a football player. But you, as an artist, and he, as a football player, *think*. The football player and the artist suffer, are anxious, have great pain, disappointment, apprehension; one believes in god and the other doesn't believe in god, one has faith and the other has no faith, but this is common to all human beings, though each one may think he is different. You may think my sorrow is entirely different from another's, that my loneliness, my desperation, are wholly opposite to another's. Our tradition is that, our conditioning is that, we are educated to that — I am an Arab, you are a Jew, and so on. And from this division there arises not only individuality but the communal racial difference. The individual identifying himself with a community, with a nation, with a race, with a religion invariably brings conflict between human beings. It is a natural law. But we are only concerned with the effects, not with the causes of war, causes of this division.

'So we are merely pointing out, not asserting, not concluding, that you, sir, are the rest of humanity, psychologically, deeply. Your reactions are shared by all humanity. Your brain is not yours, it has evolved through centuries of time. You may be conditioned as a Christian, believe in various dogmas, rituals; another has his own god, his own rituals, but all this is put together by thought. So we are questioning deeply whether there is an individual at all. We are the whole of humanity; we are the rest of mankind. This is not a romantic, fantastic, statement, and it is important, necessary, when we are going to talk over together the meaning of death.

'What do you say to all this, sir?'

'I must say I am rather puzzled by all these questions. I am not certain why I have always considered myself to be separate from you or from somebody else. What you say seems to be true but I must think it over, I must have a little time to assimilate all that you have said so far.'

'Time is the enemy of perception. If you are going to think over what we have talked about so far, argue with yourself, discuss what has been said, analyse what we have talked over together, it is going to take time. And time is a brand new factor in the perception of that which is true. Anyhow, shall we leave it for the moment?'

He came back after a couple of days and he seemed more quiet and rather concerned. It was a cloudy morning and probably it was going to rain. In this part of the world they need much more rain because beyond the hills there is a vast desert. It gets very cold here at night because of that.

30

'I have come back after a couple of days of quiet thinking. I have a house by the sea, I live by myself. It is one of those little seaside cottages and you have in front of you the beach and the blue Pacific, and you can walk for miles on the beach. I generally go for long walks either in the morning or evening. After seeing you the other day I took a walk along the beach, probably about five miles or more, and I decided to come back and see you again. I was at first very disturbed. I couldn't quite make out what you were saying, what you were pointing out to me. Though I am rather a sceptical person about these matters, I allowed what you were saying to occupy my mind. It wasn't that I was inwardly accepting or denying it, but it intrigued me, and I purposely use the word "allow" — to allow it to enter into my mind. And after some deliberation I took a car and drove along by the coast and then turned inland and came here. It is a beautiful valley. I am glad to find you here. So could we continue with what we were talking about the other day?

'If I understand it clearly, you were pointing out that tradition, long conditioned thinking, can bring about a fixation, a concept that one readily accepts, perhaps not with a great deal of thought — accepts the idea that we are separate individuals; and as I thought more about it — I am using the word "thought" in its ordinary sense, thinking, rationalizing, questioning, arguing — it was as though I was having a discussion with myself, a prolonged dialogue, and I think I really do grasp what is involved in that. I see what we have done with the marvellous world we live in. I see the whole historical sequence. And after considerable to and fro of thought I really do understand the depth and the truth of what you said. So if you have time I would like to go much further into all this. I really came to find out, as you know, about death, but I see the importance of beginning with one's comprehension of oneself, and through the door of the self — if one can use the word — come to the question of what is death.'

'As we were saying the other day, we share, all humanity shares, the sunlight [he had not said this]; that sunlight is not

31

yours or mine. It is the life-giving energy which we all share. The beauty of a sunset, if you are watching it sensitively, is shared by all human beings. It is not yours setting in the west, east, north or south; it is the sunset that is important. And our consciousness, in which is included our reactions and actions, our ideas and concepts and patterns, systems of belief, ideologies, fears, pleasures, faith, the worship of something which we have projected, our sorrows, our griefs and pain — all this is shared by all human beings. When we suffer we have made it into a personal affair. We shut out all the suffering of mankind. Like pleasure; we treat pleasure as a private thing, ours, the excitement of it and so on. We forget that man — including woman, of course, which we needn't repeat — that man has suffered from time beyond all measure. And that suffering is the ground on which we all stand. It is shared by all human beings.

'So our consciousness is not actually yours or mine; it is the consciousness of man, evolved, grown, accumulated through many, many centuries. In that consciousness is the faith, the gods, all the rituals man has invented. It is really an activity of thought; it is thought that has made the content — behaviour, action, culture, aspiration; the whole activity of man is the activity of thought. And this consciousness is the self, is the "me", the I, the ego, the personality and so on. I think it is necessary to understand this very deeply, not merely argumentatively, logically but deeply, as blood is in all of us, is part of us, is the essence, the natural process of all human beings. When one realizes this our responsibility becomes extraordinarily important. We are responsible for everything that is happening in the world as long as the content of our consciousness continues. As long as fear, nationalities, the urge for success, you know the whole business of it — as long as that exists we are part of humanity, part of the human movement.

'This is utterly important to understand. It is so: the self is put together by thought. Thought is not, as we have said, yours or mine; thinking is not individual thinking. Thinking is shared by all human beings. And when one has really deeply seen the significance of this, then I think we can understand the nature of what it means to die.

'As a boy you must have followed a small stream gurgling along a narrow little valley, the waters running faster and faster, and have thrown something, such as a piece of stick, into the stream and followed it, down a slope, over a little mound, through a little crevasse — followed it until it went over the waterfall and disappeared. This disappearance is our life.

'What does death mean? What is the very word, the threatening feeling about it? We never seem to accept it.'

Wednesday, March 16, 1983
(Continuing the dialogue of the 15th)

'MAN HAS KILLED man in different states of mind. He has killed him for religious reasons, he has killed him for patriotic reasons, for peace, killed him through organized war. This has been our lot, killing each other endlessly.

'Sir, have you considered this kind of killing, what sorrow has come to man — the immense sorrow of mankind which has gone on through the ages, the tears, the agony, the brutality, the fear of it all? And it is still going on. The world is sick. The politicians, whether left, right, centre, or totalitarian, are not going to bring about peace. Each one of us is responsible, and being responsible we must see that the slaughter comes to an end so that we live on this earth, which is ours, in beauty and peace. It is an immense tragedy which we do not face or want to resolve. We leave it all to the experts; and the danger of experts is as dangerous as a deep precipice or a poisonous snake.

'So leaving all that aside, what is the meaning of death? What to you, sir, does death mean?'

'To me it means that all I have been, all that I am, suddenly comes to an end through some disease, accident or old age. Of course I have read and talked to Asiatics, to Indians, for whom there is a belief in reincarnation. I don't know whether this is true or not, but as far as I can understand, death means the ending of a living thing; the death of a tree, the death of a fish, death of a spider, death of my wife and children, a sudden cutting off, a sudden ending of that which has been living with all its memories, ideas, pain, anxiety, joys, pleasures, seeing the sunset together — all that has come to an end. And the remembrance of all that, not only brings tears but also the realization of one's own

34

inadequacy, one's own loneliness. And the idea of separation from one's wife and children, from the things that one has worked for, cherished, remembered, held on to, the attachments and the pain of attachment — all that and more ceases suddenly. I think we generally mean that; death means that. It is to me the ending.

'There's a picture of my wife and the children on the piano in my cottage by the sea. We used to play the piano together. There is the remembrance of them in the picture on the piano, but the actuality has gone. Remembrance is painful, or remembrance may give one pleasure, but the pleasure is rather fading because sorrow is overriding. All that to me means death.

'We had a very nice Persian cat, a very beautiful thing. And one morning it had gone. It was on the front porch. It must have eaten something — there it was, lifeless, meaningless; it will never purr again. That is death. The ending of a long life, or the ending of a new born baby. I had a small new plant once which promised to grow into a healthy tree. But some thoughtless, unobservant person passed by, trod on it, and it will never be a great tree. That is also a form of death. The ending of a day, a day that has been poor or rich and beautiful, can also be called death. The beginning and the ending.'

'Sir, what is living? From the moment one is born until one dies, what is living? It is very important to understand the way we live — why we live this way after so many centuries. It is up to you, is it not, sir, if it is one constant struggle? Conflict, pain, joy, pleasure, anxiety, loneliness, depression, and working, working, working, labouring for others or for oneself; being self-centred and perhaps occasionally generous, envious, angry, trying to suppress the anger, letting that anger go rampant, and so on. This is what we call living — tears, laughter, sorrow, and the worship of something that we have invented; living with lies, illusions and hatred, the weariness of it all, the boredom, the inanities: this is our life. Not only yours but the life of all human beings on this earth, hoping to escape from it all. This process of worship, agony, fear has gone on from the ancient of days until now — labour, strife, pain, uncertainty, confusion, and joy and laughter. All this is part of our existence.

'The ending of all this is called death. Death puts an end to all our attachments, however superficial or however deep. The attachment of the monk, the sannyasi, the attachment of the housewife, the attachment to one's family, every form of attachment must end with death.

'There are several problems involved in this: one, the question of immortality. Is there such a thing as immortality? That is, that which is not mortal, for mortal implies that which knows death. The immortal is that which is beyond time and is totally unaware of this ending. Is the self, the "me", immortal? Or does it know death? The self can never become immortal. The "me", the I, with all its qualities is put together through time, which is thought; that self can never be immortal. One can invent an idea of immortality, an image, a god, a picture and hold to that and derive comfort from it, but that is not immortality.

'Secondly (this is a little bit more complex): is it possible to live with death? Not morbidly, not in any form of self-destructiveness. Why have we divided death from living? Death is part of our life, it is part of our existence — the dying and the living, and the living and dying. They are inseparable. The envy, the anger, the sorrow, the loneliness, and the pleasure that one has, which we call living, and this thing called death — why separate them? Why keep them miles apart? Yes, miles of time apart. We accept the death of an old man. It is natural. But when a young person dies through some accident or disease, we revolt against it. We say that it is unfair, it shouldn't be. So we are always separating life and death. This is a problem which we should question, understand — or not treat as a problem, but look at, see the inward implications of, not deceptively.

'Another question is the issue of time — the time involved in living, learning, accumulating, acting, doing, and the ending of time as we know it; the time that separates the living from the ending. Where there is separation, division, from here to there, from "what is" to "what should be", time is involved. Sustaining this division between that which is called death and that which is called life, is to me a major factor.

'When there is this division, this separation there is fear. Then there is the effort of overcoming that fear and the search for comfort, satisfaction, for a sense of continuity. (We are talking about the psychological world not the physical world or the technical world.) It is time that has put the self together and it is thought that sustains the ego, the self. If only one could really grasp the significance of time and division, the separation, psychologically, of man against man, race against race, one type of culture against another. This separation, this division, is brought about by thought and time, as living and dying. And to live a life with death means a profound change in our whole outlook on existence. To end attachment without time and motive, that is dying while living.

'Love has no time. It is not my love opposed to your love. Love is never personal; one may love another but when that love is limited, narrowed down to one person, then it ceases to be love. Where there really is love there is no division of time, thought and all the complexities of life, all the misery and confusion, the uncertainties, jealousies, anxieties involved. One has to give a great deal of attention to time and thought. Not that one must live only in the present, which would be utterly meaningless. Time is the past, modified and continuing as the future. It's a continuum and thought holds on, clings to this. It clings to something which it has itself created, put together.

'Another question is: as long as human beings represent the entire humanity — you *are* the entire humanity, not representing it, just as you are the world and the world is you — what happens when you die? When you or another die, you and the other are the manifestation of that vast stream of human action and reaction, the stream of consciousness, of behaviour

37

and so on: you are of that stream. That stream has conditioned the human mind, the human brain, and as long as we remain conditioned by greed, envy, fear, pleasure, joy and all the rest of it, we are part of this stream. Your organism may end but you are of that stream, as you are, while living, that stream itself. That stream, changing, slow at times, fast at others, deep and shallow, narrowed by both sides of the bank and breaking through the narrowness into a vast volume of water — as long as you are of that stream there is no freedom. There is no freedom from time, from the confusion and the misery of all the accumulated memories and attachments. It is only when there is the ending of that stream, the ending, not you stepping out of it and becoming something else, but the ending of it, only then is there quite a different dimension. That dimension cannot be measured by words. The ending without a motive is the whole significance of dying and living. The roots of heaven are in living and dying.'

THE CLOUDS WERE very low this morning. It rained last night, not too much but it has left the earth watered, rich, nourished. Considering, on a morning like this with the hills floating among the clouds and with those skies, the enormous energy that man has expended on this earth, the vast technological progress in the last fifty years, all the rivers more or less polluted and the waste of energy in this everlasting entertainment, it all seems so strange and so sick.

On the veranda this morning time is not very near to man, time as movement, time as going from here to there, time to learn, time to act, time as a means of changing from this to that in the ordinary things of life. One can understand that time is necessary to learn a language, to learn a skill, to build an aeroplane, to put together a computer, to travel around the world; the time of youth, the time of old age, time as the setting of the sun and of the sun rising slowly over the hills, the long shadows and the growth of a slowly maturing tree, time to become a good gardener, a good carpenter and so on. In the physical world, in physical action, time to learn becomes necessary and useful.

Is it that we carry over, extend, the same usage of time into the psychological world? Extend this way of thinking, acting, learning into the world inside the skin, into the area of the psyche, as hope, as becoming something, as self-improvement? It sounds rather absurd — the changing from this to that, from 'what is' to 'what should be'. Time is necessary, one thinks, to change the whole complex quality of violence into that which is not violent.

Sitting quietly by yourself, overlooking the valley, wide and long, you could almost count the rows of orange trees, the beautifully kept orchards. Seeing the beauty of the earth, of the valley, does not involve time, but the translation of that perception on to a canvas or into a poem needs time. Perhaps we use time as a means of escaping from 'what is', from what we are, from what the future will be for ourselves and for the rest of mankind.

Time in the psychological realm is the enemy of man. We want the psyche to evolve, grow, expand, fulfil, turn itself into something more than what it is. We never question the validity of such a desire, of such a concept; we easily, perhaps happily, accept that the psyche can evolve, flourish, and that one day there will be peace and happiness. But actually there is no psychological evolution.

There is a humming bird going from flower to flower, brightness in this quiet light, with such vitality in that little thing. The rapidity of the wings, so fantastically rhythmical, steady; it seems it can move forward and backward. It is a marvellous thing to watch it, to feel the delicacy, the bright colour, and wonder at its beauty, so small, so rapid and so quickly gone. And there is a mocking bird on the telephone wire. Another bird is sitting on the top of that tree overlooking the whole world. It has been there for over half an hour, never moving, but watching, moving its little head to see that there is no danger. And it too has gone now. The clouds are beginning to move away from the hills, and how green the hills are.

As we were saying, there is no psychological evolution. The psyche can never become or grow into something which it is not. Conceit and arrogance cannot grow into better and more conceit, nor can selfishness, which is the common lot of all human beings, become more and more selfish, more and more of its own nature. It is rather frightening to realize that the very word 'hope' contains the whole world of the future. This movement from 'what is' to 'what should be' is an illusion, is really, if one can use the word, a lie. We accept what man has repeated throughout the ages as a matter of fact, but when we begin to question, doubt, we can see very clearly, if we want to see it and not hide behind some image or some fanciful verbal structure, the nature and the structure of the psyche, the ego, the 'me'. The 'me' can never become a better me. It will attempt to, it thinks it can, but the 'me' remains in subtle forms. The self hides in many garments, in many structures; it varies from time to time, but there is always this self, this separative, self-centred activity which imagines that one day it will make itself something which it is not.

So one sees there is no becoming of the self, there is only the ending of selfishness, of anxiety, of pain and sorrow which are the content of the psyche, of the 'me'. There is only the ending of all that, and that ending does not require time. It isn't that it will all end the day after tomorrow. It will only end when there is the perception of its movement. To perceive not only objectively, without any prejudice, bias, but to perceive without all the accumulations of the past; to witness all this without the watcher — the watcher is of time and however much he may want to bring about a mutation in himself, he will always be the watcher; remembrances, however pleasurable, have no reality, they are things of the past, gone, finished, dead: only in observing without the observer, who is the past, does one see the nature of time and the ending of time.

The humming bird has come back again. A ray of sunlight through the broken clouds has caught it, flashing its colours and the long thin beak and the rapidity of those wings. The pure watching of that little bird, without any reaction, just watching it, is to watch the whole world of beauty.

'I heard you the other day saying that time is the enemy of man. You explained something briefly about it. It seems such an outrageous statement. And you have made other similar statements. Some of them I have found to be true, natural, but one's mind never easily sees that which is actual, the truth, the fact. I was asking myself, and I have asked others too, why our minds have become so dull, so slow, why we cannot instantly see whether something is false or true? Why do we need explanations which seem so obvious when you have explained them? Why don't I, and any of us, see the truth of this fact? What has happened to our minds? I would like, if I may, to have a dialogue about it with you, to find out why my mind isn't subtle, quick. And can this mind, which has been trained and educated, ever become really, deeply, subtle, rapid, seeing something instantly, the quality and the truth or the falseness of it?'

'Sir, let's begin to enquire why we have become like this. It surely has nothing to do with old age. Is it the way of our life — the drinking, the smoking, the drugs, the bustle, the weariness, the everlasting occupation? Outwardly and inwardly we are occupied with something. Is it the very nature of knowledge? We are trained to acquire knowledge — through college, university, or in doing something skilfully. Is knowledge one of the factors of this lack of subtlety? Our brains are filled with so many facts, they have gathered so much information, from the television and from every newspaper and magazine, and they are recording as much as they can; they are absorbing, holding. So is knowledge one of the factors that destroys subtlety? But you can't get rid of your knowledge or put it aside; you have to have knowledge. Sir, you have to have knowledge to drive a car, to write a letter, to carry out various transactions; you even have to have some kind of knowledge of how to hold a spade. Of course you do. We have to have knowledge in the world of everyday activity.

'But we are speaking of the knowledge accumulated in the psychological world, the knowledge that you have gathered about your wife, if you have a wife; that very knowledge of having lived with your wife for ten days or fifty years has dulled your brain, has it not? The memories, the pictures are all stored there. We are talking of this kind of inward knowledge.

42

Knowledge has its own superficial subtleties: when to yield, when to resist, when to gather and when not to gather, but we are asking: doesn't that very knowledge make your mind, your brain, mechanical, repetitious from habit? The encylopaedia has all the knowledge of all the people who have written in it. Why not leave that knowledge on the shelf and use it when necessary? Don't carry it in your brain.

'We are asking: does that knowledge prevent the instant comprehension, instant perception, which brings about mutation, the subtlety that isn't in the words? Is it that we are conditioned by the newspapers, by the society in which we live — which, by the way, we have created, for every human being from past generations to the present has created this society whether in this part of the world or any other part? Is it conditioning by religions that has shaped our thinking? When you have strong beliefs in some figure, in some image, that very strength prevents the subtlety, the quickness.

'Are we so constantly occupied that there is no space in our mind and heart — space both outwardly and inwardly? We need a little space, but you cannot have space physically if you are in a crowded city, or crowded in your family, crowded by all the impressions you have received, all the pressures. And psychologically there must be space — not the space that thought may imagine, not the space of isolation, not the space that divides human beings, politically, religiously, racially, not the space between continents, but an inward space that has no centre. Where there is a centre there is a periphery, there is a circumference. We are not talking of such space.

'And is another reason why we are not subtle, quick, because we have become specialists? We may be quick in our own specialization, but one wonders, if one is trained, specialized, whether there is any comprehension of the nature of sorrow, pain, loneliness and so on. Of course you cannot be trained to have a good, clear mind; the word "trained" is to be conditioned. And how can a conditioned mind ever be clear?

'So all these may be the factors, sir, that prevent us from having a good, subtle, clear mind.'

'Thank you, sir, for seeing me. Perhaps, and I hope that, some of what you have said — not that I have understood it completely — but that some of the things you have said may take seed in me and that I will allow that seed to grow, to flourish without interfering with it. Perhaps then I may see something very rapidly, comprehend something without tremendous explanations, verbal analysis and so on. Good bye, sir.'

AT THE BIRD feeder there were a dozen or more birds chirping away, pecking at the grains, struggling, fighting each other, and when another big bird came they all fluttered away. When the big bird left again they all came back, chattering, quarrelling, chirping, making quite a lot of noise. Presently a cat went by and there was a flurry, a screeching and a great to do. The cat was chased away — it was one of those wild cats, not a pet cat; there are a great many of those wild ones around here of different sizes, shapes and colours. At the feeder all day long there were birds, little ones and big ones, and then a blue-jay came scolding everybody, the whole universe, and chased the other birds away — or rather they left when it came. They were very watchful for cats. And as the evening drew close all the birds went away and there was silence, quiet, peaceful. The cats came and went, but there were no birds.

That morning the clouds were full of light and there was promise in the air of more rain. For the past few weeks it had been raining. There is an artificial lake and the waters were right to the top. All the green leaves and the shrubs and the tall trees were waiting for the sun, which hadn't appeared bright as the Californian sun is; it had not shown its face for many a day.

One wonders what is the future of mankind, the future of all those children you see shouting, playing — such happy, gentle, nice faces — what is their future? The future is what we are now. This has been so historically for many thousands of years — the living and dying, and all the travail of our lives. We don't seem to pay much attention to the future. You see on television endless entertainment from morning until late in the night, except for

45

one or two channels, but they are very brief and not too serious. The children are entertained. The commercials all sustain the feeling that you are being entertained. And this is happening practically all over the world. What will be the future of these children? There is the entertainment of sport — thirty, forty thousand people watching a few people in the arena and shouting themselves hoarse. And you also go and watch some ceremony being performed in a great cathedral, some ritual, and that too is a form of entertainment, only you call that holy, religious, but it is still an entertainment — a sentimental, romantic experience, a sensation of religiosity. Watching all this in different parts of the world, watching the mind being occupied with amusement, entertainment, sport, one must inevitably ask, if one is in any way concerned: what is the future? More of the same in different forms? A variety of amusements?

So you have to consider, if you are at all aware of what is happening to you, how the worlds of entertainment and sport are capturing your mind, shaping your life. Where is all this leading to? Or perhaps you are not concerned at all? You probably don't care about tomorrow. Probably you haven't given it thought, or, if you have, you may say it is too complex, too frightening, too dangerous to think of the coming years — not of your particular old age but of the destiny, if we can use that word, the result of our present way of life, filled with all kinds of romantic, emotional, sentimental feelings and pursuits, and the whole world of entertainment impinging on your mind. If you are at all aware of all this, what is the future of mankind?

As we said earlier, the future is what you are now. If there is no change — not superficial adaptations, superficial adjustments to any pattern, political, religious or social, but the change that is far deeper, demanding your attention, your care, your affection — if there is not a fundamental change, then the future is what we are doing every day of our life in the present. Change is rather a difficult word. Change to what? Change to another pattern? To another concept? To another political or religious system?

Change from this to that? That is still within the realm, or within the field of 'what is'. Change to that is projected by thought, formulated by thought, materialistically determined.

So one must enquire carefully into this word change. Is there a change if there is a motive? Is there a change if there is a particular direction, a particular end, a conclusion that seems sane, rational? Or perhaps a better phrase is 'the ending of what is'. The ending, not the movement of 'what is' to 'what should be'. That is not change. But the ending, the cessation, the — what is the right word? — I think ending is a good word so let's stick to that. The ending. But if the ending has a motive, a purpose, is a matter of decision, then it is merely a change from this to that. The word decision implies the action of will. 'I will do this'; 'I won't do that'. When desire enters into the act of the ending, that desire becomes the cause of ending. Where there is a cause there is a motive and so there is no real ending at all.

The twentieth century has had a tremendous lot of changes produced by two devastating wars, and the dialectical materialism, and the scepticism of religious beliefs, activities and rituals and so on, apart from the technological world which has brought about a great many changes, and there will be further changes when the computer is fully developed — you are just at the beginning of it. Then when the computer takes over, what is going to happen to our human minds? That is a different question which we should go into another time.

When the industry of entertainment takes over, as it is gradually doing now, when the young people, the students, the children, are constantly instigated to pleasure, to fancy, to romantic sensuality, the words restraint and austerity are pushed away, never even given a thought. The austerity of the monks, the sannyasis, who deny the world, who clothe their bodies with some kind of uniform or just a cloth — this denial of the material world is surely not austerity. You probably won't even listen to this, to what the implications of austerity are. When you have been brought up from childhood to amuse yourself and escape from yourself through entertainment, religious or otherwise, and when most of the psychologists say that you must express everything you feel and that any form of holding back or restraint is detrimental, leading to various forms of neuroticism, you naturally enter more and more into the world of sport, amusement, entertainment, all helping you to escape from yourself, from what you are.

The understanding of the nature of what you are, without any distortions, without any bias, without any reactions to what you discover you are, is the beginning of austerity. The watching, the awareness, of every thought, every feeling, not to restrain it, not to control it, but to watch it, like watching a bird in flight, without any of your own prejudices and distortions — that watching brings about an extraordinary sense of austerity that goes beyond all restraint, all the fooling around with oneself and all this idea of self-improvement, self-fulfilment. That is all rather childish. In this watching there is great freedom and in that freedom there is the sense of the dignity of austerity. But if you said all this to a modern group of students or children, they would probably look out of the window in boredom because this world is bent on its own pursuit of pleasure.

A large fawn-coloured squirrel came down the tree and went up to the feeder, nibbled at a few grains, sat there on top of it, looked around with its large beady eyes, its tail up, curved, a marvellous thing. It sat there for a moment or so, came down, went along the few rocks and then dashed to the tree and up, and disappeared.

It appears that man has always escaped from himself, from what he is, from where he is going, from what all this is about — the universe, our daily life, the dying and the beginning. It is strange that we never realize that however much we may escape from ourselves, however much we may wander away consciously, deliberately or unconsciously, subtly, the conflict, the pleasure, the pain, the fear and so on are always there. They ultimately dominate. You may try to suppress them, you may try to put them away deliberately with an act of will but they surface again. And pleasure is one of the factors that predominate; it too has the same conflicts, the same pain, the same boredom. The weariness of pleasure and the fret is part of this turmoil of our life. You can't escape it, my friend. You can't escape from this deep unfathomed turmoil unless you really give thought to it, not only thought but see by careful attention, diligent watching, the whole movement of thought and the self. You may say all this is too tiresome, perhaps unnecessary. But if you do not pay attention to this, give heed, the future is not only going to be more destructive, more intolerable but without much significance. All this is not a dampening, depressing point of view, it is actually so. What you are now is what you will be in the coming days. You can't avoid it. It is as definite as the sun rising and setting. This is the share of all man, of all humanity, unless we all change, each one of us, change to something that is not projected by thought.

IT IS THE second day of a spring morning. It's lovely. It is extraordinarily beautiful here. It rained last night heavily and everything is again washed clean and all the leaves are shining bright in the sunlight. There is a scent in the air of many flowers and the sky is blue, dotted with passing clouds. The beauty of such a morning is timeless. It isn't this morning: it is the morning of the whole world. It is the morning of a thousand yesterdays. It is the morning that one hopes will continue, will last endlessly. It is a morning that is full of soft sunlight, sparkling, clear, and the air is so pure here, fairly high up the valley. The orange trees and the bright yellow oranges have been washed clean and they are shining as though it was the first morning of their birth. The earth is heavy with the rain and there is snow on the high mountains. It is really a timeless morning.

Across the valley the far mountains enclosing this valley are eager for the sun, for it has been a cold night, and all the rocks and the pebbles and the little stream seem to be aware and full of life.

You sit quietly far from everything and look at the blue sky, feel the whole earth, the purity and the loveliness of everything that lives and moves on this earth—except man of course. Man is what he is now after many thousands of centuries of time. And he will go on perhaps in the same manner; what he is now is what he will be tomorrow and a thousand tomorrows. Time, evolution, has brought him to what he is now. The future is what he is unless, of course, there is a deep abiding mutation of his whole psyche.

Time has become extraordinarily important to man, to all of us —time to learn, time to have a skill, time to become and time to die, time both outwardly in the physical world and time in the psychological world. It is necessary to have time to learn a

50

language, to learn how to drive, to learn how to speak, to acquire knowledge. If you had no time you couldn't put things together to bring about a house; you must have time to lay brick upon brick. You must have time to go from here to where you want to go. Time is an extraordinary factor in our life — to acquire, to dispense, to be healed, to write a simple letter. And we seem to think we need psychological time, the time of what has been, modified now and continuing in the future. Time is the past, the present and the future. Man inwardly pins his hope on time; hope is time, the future, the endless tomorrows, time to *become* inwardly — one *is* 'this', one will *become* 'that'. The becoming, as in the physical world, from the little operator to the big operator, from the nonentity to the highest in some profession — to become.

We think we need time to change from 'this' to 'that'. The very words 'change' and 'hope' intrinsically imply time. One can understand that time is necessary to travel, to reach a port, to reach land after a long flight to the desired place. The desired place is the future. That is fairly obvious and time is necessary in that realm of achieving, gaining, becoming proficient in some profession, in a career that demands training. There, time seems not only necessary but must exist. And in the world of the psyche this same movement, this becoming, is extended. But is there psychological becoming at all? We never question that. We have accepted it as natural. The religions, the evolutionary books, have informed us that we need time to change from 'what is' to 'what should be'. The distance covered is time. And we have accepted that there is a certain pleasure and pain in becoming non-violent when one is violent, that to achieve the ideal needs an enormous amount of time. And we have followed this pattern all the days of our life, blindly, never questioning. We don't doubt. We follow the old traditional pattern. And perhaps that is one of the miseries of man — the hope of fulfilment, and the pain that that fulfilment, that hope, is not achieved, is not come by easily.

Is there actually time in the psychological world — that is, to change that which *is* to something totally different? Why do ideals, ideologies, whether political or religious, exist at all? Is it not one of the divisive concepts of man that has brought about conflict? After all, the ideologies, the left, right or centre, are put together by study, by the activity of thought, weighing, judging, and coming to a conclusion, and so shutting the door on all fuller enquiry. Ideologies have existed perhaps as long as man can remember. They are like belief or faith that separate man from man. And this separation comes about through time. The 'me', the I, the ego, the person, from the family to the group, to the tribe, to the nation. One wonders if the tribal divisions can ever be bridged over. Man has tried to unify nations, which are really glorified tribalism. You cannot unify nations. They will always remain separate. Evolution has separate groups. We maintain wars, religious and otherwise. And time will not change this. Knowledge, experience, definite conclusions, will never bring about that global comprehension, global relationship, a global mind.

So the question is: is there a possibility of bringing about a change in 'what is', the actuality, totally disregarding the movement of time? Is there a possibility of changing violence — not by becoming non-violent, that is merely the opposite of 'what is'? The opposite of 'what is' is merely another movement of thought. Our question is: can envy, with all its implications, be changed without time being involved at all, knowing that the word change itself implies time — not even transformed, for the very word transform means to move from one form to another form — but to radically end envy without time?

Time is thought. Time is the past. Time is motive. Without any motive can there be — and we will use the word — change? Does not the very word motive already imply a direction, a conclusion? And when there is a motive there is actually no change at all. Desire is again a rather complex thing, complex in its structure. Desire to bring about a change, or the will to change, becomes the motive and therefore that motive distorts that which has to be changed, that which has to end. The ending has no time.

Clouds are slowly gathering around the mountain, clouds are moving to blot out the sun and probably it will rain again, as yesterday. For here in this part of the world it is the season of rain. It never rains in the summer time; when it is hot and dry, this valley is desert. Beyond the hills the desert lies out there, open, endless and bleak. And at other times it is very beautiful, so vast in its space. The very vastness of it makes it a desert. When the spring disappears it gets hotter and hotter and the trees seem to wither and the flowers have gone and the dry heat makes all things clean again.

'Why do you say, sir, that time is unnecessary for change?'

'Let us together find out what is the truth of the matter, not accepting what one has said, or disagreeing, but together have a dialogue to explore into this matter. One is trained to believe and it is the tradition that time is necessary for change. That is correct, is it not? Time is used to become from what one is to something greater, to something more. We are not talking about the physical time, the time necessary to gain a physical skill, but rather we are considering whether the psyche can become more than what it is, better than what it is, reach a higher state of consciousness. That is the whole movement of measurement, comparison. Together we are asking, are we not, what does change imply? We live in disorder, confused, uncertain, reacting against this and for that. We are seeking reward and avoiding punishment. We want to be secure, yet everything we do seems to bring about insecurity. This, and more, brings about disorder in our daily life. You can't be disordered in business, for example, or negligent. You have to be precise, think clearly, logically. But we do not carry that same attitude into the psychological world. We have this constant urge to move away

53

from "what is", to become something other than the understanding of "what is", to avoid the causes of disorder.'

'That I understand,' the questioner said. 'We do escape from "what is". We never consider carefully, diligently, what is going on, what is happening now in each one of us. We do try to suppress or transcend "what is". If we have a great deal of pain, psychologically, inwardly, we never look at it carefully. We want immediately to erase it, to find some consolation. And always there is this struggle to reach a state where there is no pain, where there is no disorder. But the very attempt to bring about order seems to increase disorder, or bring about other problems.'

'I do not know if you have noticed that when the politicians try to resolve one problem, that very resolution multiplies other problems. This again is going on all the time.'

'Are you saying, sir, that time is not a factor of change? I can vaguely comprehend this but I am not quite sure I really understand it. You are saying in fact that if I have a motive for change, that very motive becomes a hindrance to change, because that motive is my desire, my urge to move away from that which is unpleasant or disturbing to something much more satisfactory, which will give me greater happiness. So a motive or a cause has already dictated, or shaped the end, the psychological end. This I understand. I am getting a glimmer of what you are saying. I am beginning to feel the implication of change without time.'

'So let us ask the question: is there a timeless perception of that "which is"? That is, to look at, to observe "what is" without the past, without all the accumulated memories, the names, the words, the reactions — to look at that feeling, at that reaction, which we call, let us say, envy. To observe this feeling without

54

the actor, the actor who is all the remembrance of things that have happened before.

'Time is not merely the rising of the sun and the setting, or yesterday, today and tomorrow. Time is much more complicated, more intricate, subtle. And really to understand the nature and the depth of time one has to meditate upon whether time has a stop — not fictitious time nor the imagination that conjures up so many fantastic, romantic probabilities — but whether time, really, actually, in the field of the psyche, can ever come to an end? That is really the question. One can analyse the nature of time, investigate it, and try to find out whether the continuity of the psyche is a reality or the desperate hope of man to cling to something that will give him some sort of security, comfort. Does time have its roots in heaven? When you look at the heavens, the planets and the unimaginable number of stars, can that universe be understood by the time-bound quality of the mind? Is time necessary to grasp, to understand, the whole movement of the cosmos and of the human being — to see instantly that which is always true?

'One should really, if one may point out, hold it in your mind, not think about it, but just observe the whole movement of time, which is really the movement of thought. Thought and time are not two different things, two different movements, actions. Time is thought and thought is time. Is there, to put it differently, the total ending of thought? That is, the ending of knowledge? Knowledge is time, thought is time, and we are asking whether this accumulating process of knowledge, gathering more and more information, pursuing more and more the intricacies of existence, can end? Can thought, which is after all the essence of the psyche, the fears, the pleasures, the anxieties, the loneliness, the sorrow and the concept of the I — I as separate from another — this self-centred activity of selfishness, can all that come to an end? When death comes there is the ending of all that. But we are not talking about death, the final ending, but whether we can actually perceive that thought, time, have an ending.

'Knowledge after all is the accumulation through time of various experiences, the recording of various incidents, happenings, and so on; this recording is naturally stored in the brain, this recording is the essence of time. Can we find out when recording is necessary, and whether psychological recording is necessary at all? It is not dividing the necessary knowledge and skill, but beginning to understand the nature of recording, why human beings record and from that recording react and act. When one is insulted or psychologically hurt by a word, by a gesture, by an action, why should that hurt be recorded? Is it possible not to record the flattery or the insult so that the psyche is never cluttered up, so that it has vast space, and the psyche that we are conscious of as the "me", which again is put together by thought and time, comes to an end? We are always afraid of something that we have never seen, perceived — something not experienced. You can't experience truth. To experience there must be the experiencer. The experiencer is the result of time, accumulated memory, knowledge and so on.

'As we said at the beginning, time demands quick, watchful, attentive understanding. In our daily life can we exist without the concept of the future? Not concept — forgive me, not the word concept — but can one live without time, inwardly? The roots of heaven are not in time and thought.'

'Sir, what you say has actually, in daily life, become a reality. Your various statements about time and thought seem now, while I am listening to you, so simple, so clear, and perhaps for a second or two there is the ending and stopping of time. But when I go back to my ordinary routine, the weariness and the boredom of it all, even pleasure becomes rather wearisome — when I go back I will pick up the old threads. It seems so extraordinarily difficult to let go of the threads and look, without reaction, at the way of time. But I am beginning to understand (and I hope it is not only verbally) that there is a possibility of not recording, if I may use your word. I realize I am the record. I have been

56

programmed to be this or that. One can see that fairly easily and perhaps put all that aside. But the ending of thought and the intricacies of time need a great deal of observation, a great deal of investigation. But who is to investigate, for the investigator himself is the result of time? I catch something. You are really saying; just watch without any reaction, give total attention to the ordinary things of life and there discover the possibility of ending time and thought. Thank you indeed for this interesting talk.'

IT HAD BEEN raining all day and the clouds hung low over the valley and the hills and the mountains. You couldn't see the hills at all. It is a rather gloomy morning but there are new leaves, new flowers, and the little things are growing fast. It is spring and there is all this cloud and gloom. The earth is recovering from the winter and in this recovery there is great beauty. It has been raining almost every day for the last month and a half; there have been great storms and winds, destroying many houses and land sliding down the hillside. All along the coast there is great destruction. In this part of the country everything seems to have been so extravagant. It is never the same from winter to winter. One winter you may have hardly any rain, and in other winters there may be most destructive rain, huge monstrous waves, the roads awash, and though it was spring the elements were never graceful with the land.

There are demonstrations all over the country against particular kinds of war, against nuclear destruction. There are pros and cons. The politicians talk about defence, but actually there is no defence; there is only war, there is only killing millions of people. This is rather a difficult situation. It is a great problem which man is facing. One side wants to expand in its own way, the other is aggressively pushing, selling arms, bringing about certain definite ideologies and invading lands.

Man is now posing a question he should have put to himself many years ago, not at the last moment. He has been preparing for wars all the days of his life. Preparation for war seems unfortunately to be our natural tendency. Having come a long way along that path we are now saying: what shall we do? What

58

are we human beings to do? Actually facing the issue, what is our responsibility? This is what is really facing our present humanity, not what kinds of instruments of war we should invent and build. We always bring about a crisis and then ask ourselves what to do. Given the situation as it is now, the politicians and the vast general public will decide with their national, racial, pride, with their fatherlands and motherlands and all the rest of it.

The question is too late. The question we must put to ourselves, in spite of the immediate action to be taken, is whether it is possible to stop all wars, not a particular kind of war, the nuclear or the orthodox, and find out most earnestly what are the causes of war. Until those causes are discovered, dissolved, whether we have conventional war or the nuclear form of war, we will go on and man will destroy man.

So we should really ask: what are essentially, fundamentally, the causes of war? See together the true causes, not invented, not romantic, patriotic causes and all that nonsense, but actually see why man prepares to murder legally — war. Until we research and find the answer, wars will go on. But we are not seriously enough considering, or committed to, the uncovering of the causes of war. Putting aside what we are now faced with, the immediacy of the issue, the present crisis, can we not together discover the true causes and put them aside, dissolve them? This needs the urge to find the truth.

Why is there, one must ask, this division — the Russian, the American, the British, the French, the German and so on — why is there this division between man and man, between race and race, culture against culture, one series of ideologies against another? Why? Why is there this separation? Man has divided the earth as yours and mine — why? Is it that we try to find security, self-protection, in a particular group, or in a particular belief, faith? For religions also have divided man, put man against man — the Hindus, the Muslims, the Christians, the Jews and so on. Nationalism, with its unfortunate patriotism, is really

59

a glorified form, an enobled form, of tribalism. In a small tribe or in a very large tribe there is a sense of being together, having the same language, the same superstitions, the same kind of political, religious system. And one feels safe, protected, happy, comforted. And for that safety, comfort, we are willing to kill others who have the same kind of desire to be safe, to feel protected, to belong to something. This terrible desire to identify oneself with a group, with a flag, with a religious ritual and so on, gives us the feeling that we have roots, that we are not homeless wanderers. There is the desire, the urge, to find one's roots.

And also we have divided the world into economic spheres, with all their problems. Perhaps one of the major causes of war is heavy industry. When industry and economics go hand in hand with politics they must inevitably sustain a separative activity to maintain their economic stature. All countries are doing this, the great and the small. The small are being armed by the big nations — some quietly, surreptitiously, others openly. Is the cause of all this misery, suffering, and the enormous waste of money on armaments, the visible sustenance of pride, of wanting to be superior to others?

It is our earth, not yours or mine or his. We are meant to live on it, helping each other, not destroying each other. This is not some romantic nonsense but the actual fact. But man has divided the earth, hoping thereby that in the particular he is going to find happiness, security, a sense of abiding comfort. Until a radical change takes place and we wipe out all nationalities, all ideologies, all religious divisions, and establish a global relationship — psychologically first, inwardly before organizing the outer — we shall go on with wars. If you harm others, if you kill others, whether in anger or by organized murder which is called war, you, who are the rest of humanity, not a separate human being fighting the rest of mankind, are destroying yourself.

This is the real issue, the basic issue, which you must

understand and resolve. Until you are committed, dedicated, to eradicating this national, economic, religious division, you are perpetuating war, you are responsible for all wars whether nuclear or traditional.

This is really a very important and urgent question: whether man, you, can bring about this change in yourself — not say. 'If I change, will it have any value? Won't it be just a drop in a vast lake and have no effect at all? What is the point of my changing?' That is a wrong question, if one may point out. It is wrong because you are the rest of mankind. You are the world, you are not separate from the world. You are not an American, Russian, Hindu or Muslim. You are apart from these labels and words, you are the rest of mankind because your consciousness, your reactions, are similar to the others. You may speak a different language, have different customs, that is superficial culture — all cultures apparently are superficial — but your consciousness, your reactions, your faith, your beliefs, your ideologies, your fears, anxieties, loneliness, sorrow and pleasure, are similar to the rest of mankind. If you change it will affect the whole of mankind.

This is important to consider — not vaguely, superficially — in enquiring into, researching, seeking out, the causes of war. War can only be understood and put an end to if you and all those who are concerned very deeply with the survival of man, feel that you are utterly responsible for killing others. What will make you change? What will make you realize the appalling situation that we have brought about now? What will make you turn your face against all division — religious, national, ethical and so on? Will more suffering? But you have had thousands upon thousands of years of suffering and man has not changed; he still pursues the same tradition, same tribalism, the same religious divisions of 'my god' and 'your god'.

The gods or their representatives are invented by thought; they have actually no reality in daily life. Most religions have said that to kill human beings is the greatest sin. Long before

61

Christianity, the Hindus said this, the Buddhists said it, yet people kill in spite of their belief in god, or their belief in a saviour and so on; they still pursue the path of killing. Will the reward of heaven change you or the punishment of hell? That too has been offered to man. And that too has failed. No external imposition, laws, systems, will ever stop the killing of man. Nor will any intellectual, romantic, conviction stop wars. They will stop only when you, as the rest of humanity, see the truth that as long as there is division in any form, there must be conflict, limited or wide, narrow or expansive, that there must be struggle, conflict, pain. So you are responsible, not only to your children, but to the rest of humanity. Unless you deeply understand this, not verbally or ideationally or merely intellectually, but feel this in your blood, in your way of looking at life, in your actions, you are supporting organized murder which is called war. The immediacy of perception is far more important than the immediacy of answering a question which is the outcome of a thousand years of man killing man.

The world is sick and there is no one outside you to help you except yourself. We have had leaders, specialists, every kind of external agency, including god — they have had no effect; they have in no way influenced your psychological state. They cannot guide you. No statesman, no teacher, no guru, no one can make you strong inwardly, supremely healthy. As long as you are in disorder, as long as your house is not kept in a proper condition, a proper state, you will create the external prophet, and he will always be misleading you. Your house is in disorder and no one on this earth or in heaven can bring about order in your house. Unless you yourself understand the nature of disorder, the nature of conflict, the nature of division, your house, that is you, will always remain in disorder, at war.

It is not a question of who has the greatest military might, but rather it is man against man, man who has put together ideologies, and these ideologies, which man has made, are against each other. Until these ideas, ideologies, end and man becomes responsible for other human beings, there cannot possibly be peace in the world.

IT IS A new day and the sun won't be up for an hour or so. It is quite dark and the trees are silent, waiting for the dawn and the sun to rise behind the hills. There ought to be a prayer for dawn. It comes so slowly, penetrating the whole world. And here in this quiet secluded house, surrounded by orange trees and a few flowers, it is extraordinarily quiet. There are no birds as yet singing their morning song. The world is asleep, at least in this part of the world, far from all civilization, from the noise, the brutality, the vulgarity and the talk of politicians.

Slowly, with great patience, the dawn begins in the deep silence of the night. It was broken by the mourning dove and the hoot of an owl. There are several owls here, they were calling to each other. And the hills and the trees are beginning to awaken. In silence the dawn begins, it gets lighter and lighter, and the dew is on the leaf and the sun is just climbing over the hill. The first rays of the sun are caught in those tall trees, in that old oak that has been there for a very, very long time. And the mourning dove begins with its soft mournful call. Across the road, across the orange trees, there is a peacock calling. Even in this part of the world there are peacocks, at least there are a few of them. And the day has begun. It is a wonderful day. It is so new, so fresh, so alive and full of beauty. It is a new day without any past remembrances, without the call of another.

There is great wonder when one looks at all the beauties — those bright oranges with the dark leaves, and the few flowers, bright in their glory. One wonders at this extraordinary light

---

*Between this date and March 31 Krishnamurti had been to New York where he gave two talks at the Felt Forum, Madison Square Garden, and attended a seminar organized by Dr David Shainberg.

which only this part of the world seems to have. One wonders as one looks at the creation which seems to have no beginning and no end — a creation not by cunning thought, but the creation of a new morning. This morning it is as it has never been before, so bright, so clear. And the blue hills are looking down. It is the creation of a new day as it has never been before.

There is a squirrel with a long bushy tail, quivering and shy in the old pepper tree which has lost many branches; it is getting very old. It must have seen many storms, as the oak has in its old age, quiet, with a great dignity. It is a new morning, full of an ancient life; it has no time, no problems. It exists and that in itself is a miracle. It is a new morning without any memory. All the past days are over, gone, and the voice of the mourning dove comes across the valley, and the sun is now over the hill, covering the earth. And it too has no yesterday. The trees in the sun and the flowers have no time. It is the miracle of a new day.

'We want continuity,' said the man. 'Continuity is part of our life. Continuity of generation after generation, of tradition, of the things we have known and remembered. We crave continuity and we must have it. Otherwise what are we? Continuity is in the very roots of our being. To be is to contirue. Death may come, there may be an end to many things but there is always the continuity. We go back to find our roots, our identity. If one has kept one's beginning as a family, probably one can trace it, generation after generation for many centuries, if one is interested in that kind of thing. The continuity of the worship of god, the continuity of ideologies, the continuity of opinions, values, judgements, conclusions — there is a continuity in all the things one has remembered. There is a continuity from the moment we are born until we die, with all the experiences, all the knowledge that man has acquired. Is it an illusion?'

'What has continuity? That oak, probably two hundred years old, has a continuity until it dies or is chopped down by man. And what is this continuity which man wants, craves for? The name, the form, the bank account, the things remembered? Memory has a continuity, remembrances of that which has been. The whole psyche is memory and nothing else. We attribute to the psyche a great many things — qualities, virtues, ignoble deeds, and the exercise of many clever acts in the outer and the inner world. And if one examines diligently, without any bias or conclusion, one begins to see that our whole existence with the vast network of memories, remembrances, the things that have happened before, all have continuity. And we cling to that desperately.'

The squirrel has come back. It has been away for a couple of hours; now it is back on the branch nibbling at something, watching, listening, extraordinarily alert and aware, alive, quivering with excitement. It comes and goes without telling you where it is going and when it is coming back. And as the day is getting warmer, the dove and the birds have gone. There are a few pigeons flying from one place to another in a group. You can hear their wings beating in the air. There used to be a fox here — one hasn't seen it for a long time. Probably it has gone away for ever. There are too many people about. There are plenty of rodents but people are dangerous. And this is a shy little squirrel and wayward as the swallow.

Although there is no continuity except memory, is there in the whole human being, in the brain, a place, a spot, an area small or vast, where memory doesn't exist at all, which memory has never touched? It is a remarkable thing to look at all this, to feel your way sanely, rationally, see the complexity and the intricacies of memory, and its continuity which is, after all, knowledge. Knowledge is always in the past, knowledge *is* the past. The past is vast accumulated memory as tradition. And when you have trodden that path diligently, sanely, you must inevitably ask: is there an area in the human brain, or in the very nature and structure of a human being, not merely in the outer world of his activities but inwardly, deep in the vast quiet recesses of his own brain, something that is not the outcome of memory, not the movement of a continuity?

The hills and the trees, the meadows and the groves, will continue as long as the earth exists unless man in his cruelty and despair destroys it all. The stream, the spring, from which it comes, have a continuity, but one never asks whether the hills and beyond the hills have their own continuity.

If there is no continuity what is there? There is nothing. One is afraid to be nothing. Nothing means not a thing — nothing put together by thought, nothing put together by memory, remembrances, nothing that you can put into words and then measure. There is most certainly, definitely, an area where the past doesn't cast a shadow, where time, the past or the future or the present, has no meaning. We have always tried to measure with words something that we don't know. What we do not know we try to understand and give it words and make it into a continuous noise. And so we clog our brain which is already clogged with past events, experiences, knowledge. We think knowledge is psychologically of great importance, but it is not. You can't ascend through knowledge; there must be an end to knowledge for the new to be. New is a word for something which has never been before. And that area cannot be understood or grasped by words or symbols: it is there beyond all remembrances.

THIS WINTER THERE has been constant rain, day after day, practically for the last three months. It is rather an extravagance of California — either it doesn't rain at all or it rains to drown the land. There have been great storms and very few sunny days. It has been raining all yesterday and this morning the clouds are low down on the hills and it is rather gloomy. All the leaves are beaten down by the rain of yesterday. The earth is very wet. The trees and that magnificent oak must be asking where the sun is.

On this particular morning with the clouds hiding the mountains and the hills almost down to the valley, what does it mean to be serious? What does it mean to have a very quiet, serious mind — or, if you will, brain? Are we ever serious? Or do we always live in a world of superficiality, walking to and fro, fighting, quarrelling, violent over something utterly trivial? What does it mean to have a brain that is very awake, not limited by its own thoughts, memories and remembrances? What does it mean to have a brain that is free from all the turmoil of life, all the pain, all the anxiety and the endless sorrow? Is it ever possible to have a totally free mind, free brain, not shaped by influences, by experience and the vast accumulation of knowledge?

Knowledge is time; learning means time. To learn to play the violin takes infinite patience, months of practice, years of dedicated concentration. Learning to acquire a skill, learning to become an athlete or to put together a good engine or to go to the moon — all this requires time. But is there anything to learn about the psyche, about what you are — all the vagaries, the intricacies of one's reactions and actions, the hope, the failure, the sorrow and joy — what is there to learn about all that? As we said, in a certain area of one's physical existence, gathering

68

knowledge and acting from that knowledge, requires time. Is it that we carry that same principle, extend that same movement of time into the psychological world? There too we say we must learn about ourselves, about our reactions, our behaviour, our elations and depressions, ideations and so on; we think that all that requires time too.

You can learn about the limited, but you cannot learn about the unlimited. And we try to learn about the whole field of the psyche, and say that needs time. But time may be an illusion in that area, it may be an enemy. Thought creates the illusion, and that illusion evolves, grows, extends. The illusion of all religious activity must have begun very, very simply, and now look where it is — with immense power, vast properties, great accumulation of art, wealth, and the religious hierarchy demanding obedience, urging you to have more faith. All that is the expansion, the cultivation and the evolution of illusion which has taken many centuries. And the psyche is the whole content of consciousness, is the memory of all things past and dead. We give such importance to memory. The psyche is memory. All tradition is merely the past. We cling to that and want to learn all about it, and think that time is necessary for that as in the other area.

I wonder if one ever asks whether time has a stop — time to become, time to fulfil? Is there anything to learn about all that? Or can one see that the whole movement of this illusory memory, which appears so real, can end? If time has a stop, then what is the relationship between that which lies beyond time and all the physical activities of the brain as memory, knowledge, remembrances, experiences? What is the relationship between the two? Knowledge and thought, as we have often said, are limited. The limited cannot possibly have any relationship with the unlimited but the unlimited can have some kind of communication with the limited, though that communication must always be limited, narrow, fragmentary.

One might ask, if one is commercially minded, what is the use of all this, what is the use of the unlimited, what can man profit by it? We always want a reward. We live on the principle of punishment and reward, like a dog which has been trained; you reward him when he obeys. And we are almost similar in the sense that we want to be rewarded for our actions, for our obedience and so on. Such demand is born out of the limited brain. The brain is the centre of thought and thought is ever limited under all circumstances. It may invent the extraordinary, theoretical, immeasurable, but its invention is always limited. That is why one has to be completely free from all the travail and toil of life and from self-centred activity for the unlimited to be.

That which is immeasurable cannot be measured by words. We are always trying to put the immeasurable into a frame of words, and the symbol is not the actual. But we worship the symbol, therefore we always live in a limited state.

So with the clouds hanging on the tree tops and all the birds quiet, waiting for the thunderstorm, this is a good morning to be serious, to question the whole of existence, to question the very gods and all human activity. Our lives are so short and during that short period there is nothing to learn about the whole field of the psyche, which is the movement of memory; we can only observe it. Observe without any movement of thought, observe without time, without past knowledge, without the observer who is the essence of the past. Just watch. Watch those clouds shaping and reshaping, watch the trees, the little birds. It is all part of life. When you watch attentively, with diligence, there is nothing to learn; there is only that vast space, silence and emptiness, which is all-consuming energy.

AT THE END of every leaf, the large leaves and the tiny leaves, there was a drop of water sparkling in the sun like an extraordinary jewel. And there was a slight breeze but that breeze didn't in any way disturb or destroy that drop on those leaves that were washed clean by the late rain. It was a very quiet morning, full of delight, peaceful, and with a sense of benediction in the air. And as we watched the sparkling light on every clean leaf, the earth became extraordinarily beautiful, in spite of all the telegraph wires and their ugly posts. In spite of all the noise of the world, the earth was rich, abiding, enduring. And though there were earthquakes here and there, most destructive, the earth was still beautiful. One never appreciates the earth unless one really lives with it, works with it, puts one's hands in the dust, lifting big rocks and stones — one never knows the extraordinary sense of being with the earth, the flowers, the gigantic trees and the strong grass and the hedges along the road.

Everything was alive that morning. As we watched, there was a sense of great joy and the heavens were blue, the sun was slowly coming out of the hills and there was light. As we watched the mocking bird on the wire, it was doing its antics, jumping high, doing a somersault, then coming down on the same spot on the wire. As we watched the bird enjoying itself, jumping in the air and then coming down circling, with its shrill cries, its enjoyment of life, only that bird existed, the watcher didn't exist. The watcher was no longer there, only the bird, grey and white, with a longish tail. That watching was without any movement of thought, watching the flurry of the bird that was enjoying itself.

We never watch for long. When we watch with great patience,

watch without any sense of the watcher, watch those birds, those droplets on the quivering leaves, the bees and the flowers and the long trail of ants, then time ceases, time has a stop. One doesn't take time to watch or have the patience to watch. One learns a great deal through watching — watching people, the way they walk, their talk, their gestures. You can see through their vanity or their negligence of their own bodies. They are indifferent, they are callous.

There was an eagle flying high in the air, circling without the beat of the wings, carried away by the air current beyond the hills and was lost. Watching, learning: learning is time but watching has no time. Or when you listen, listen without any interpretation, without any reaction, listen without any bias. Listen to that thunder in the skies, the thunder rolling among the hills. One never listens completely, there is always interruption. Watching and listening are a great art — watching and listening without any reaction, without any sense of the listener or the see-er. By watching and listening we learn infinitely more than from any book. Books are necessary, but watching and listening sharpen your senses. For, after all, the brain is the centre of all the reactions, thoughts and remembrances. But if your senses are not highly awakened you cannot really watch and listen and learn, not only how to act but about learning, which is the very soil in which the seed of goodness can grow.

When there is this simple, clear watching and listening, then there is an awareness — awareness of the colour of those flowers, red, yellow, white, of the spring leaves, the stems, so tender, so delicate, awareness of the heavens, the earth and those people who are passing by. They have been chattering along that long road, never looking at the trees, at the flowers, at the skies and the marvellous hills. They are not even aware of what is going on around them. They talk a great deal about the environment, how we must protect nature and so on, but it seems they are not aware of the beauty and the silence of the hills and the dignity of a marvellous old tree. They are not even aware of their own thoughts, their own reactions, nor are they aware of the way they walk, of their clothes. It does not mean that they are to be self-centred in their watching, in their awareness, but just be aware.

When you are aware there is a choice of what to do, what not to do, like and dislike, your biases, your fears, your anxieties, the joys which you have remembered, the pleasures that you have pursued; in all this there is choice, and we think that choice gives us freedom. We like that freedom to choose; we think freedom is necessary to choose — or, rather, that choice gives us a sense of freedom — but there is no choice when you see things very, very clearly.

And that leads us to an awareness without choice — to be aware without any like or dislike. When there is this really simple, honest, choiceless awareness it leads to another factor, which is attention. The word itself means to stretch out, to grasp, to hold on, but that is still the activity of the brain, it is in the brain. Watching, awareness, attention, are within the area of the brain, and the brain is limited — conditioned by all the ways of past generations, the impressions, the traditions and all the folly and the goodness of man. So all action from this attention is still limited, and that which is limited must inevitably bring disorder. When one is thinking about oneself from morning until night — one's own worries, one's own desires, demands and fulfilments — this self-centredness, being very, very limited, must cause friction in its relationship with another, who is also limited; there must be friction, there must be strain and disturbances of many kinds, the perpetual violence of human beings.

When one is attentive to all this, choicelessly aware, then out of that comes insight. Insight is not an act of remembrance, the continuation of memory. Insight is like a flash of light. You see with absolute clarity, all the complications, the consequences, the intricacies. Then this very insight is action, complete. In that there are no regrets, no looking back, no sense of being weighed down, no discrimination. This is pure, clear insight — perception without any shadow of doubt.

Most of us begin with certainty and as we grow older that certainty changes to uncertainty and we die with uncertainty. But if one begins with uncertainty, doubting, questioning, asking, demanding, with real doubt about man's behaviour, about all the religious rituals and their images and their symbols, then out of that doubt comes the clarity of certainty. When there is clear insight into violence, for instance, that very insight banishes all violence. That insight is outside the brain, if one can so put it. It is not of time. It is not of remembrance or of knowledge, and so that insight and its action changes the very brain cells. That insight is complete and from that completeness there can be logical, sane, rational, action.

This whole movement from watching, listening, to the thunder of insight, is one movement; it is not coming to it step by step. It is like a swift arrow. And that insight alone can uncondition the brain, not the effort of thought, which is determination, seeing the necessity for something; none of that will bring about total freedom from conditioning. All this is time and the ending of time. Man is time-bound and that bondage to time is the movement of thought. So where there is an ending to thought and to time there is total insight. Only then can there be the flowering of the brain. Only then can you have a complete relationship with the mind.

THERE IS A cabin high among the hills, somewhat isolated although there are other cabins there. The cabin was among those gigantic marvellous old trees, the sequoias.* Some of them are said to have existed from the time of the ancient Egyptians, perhaps from Rameses the Second. They are really marvellous trees. Their bark is rose-coloured and bright in the morning sunlight. These trees cannot be burnt; their bark resists fire and you can see where the old Indians built a fire round the tree; the dark mark of fire is still there. They are really quite gigantic in size, their trunks are enormous and if you sit very still under them in the morning light, with the sun among the tree tops, all the squirrels there will come up quite close to you. They are very inquisitive like the blue-jays, for there are jays too, blue, blue birds, always ready to scold you, asking why you are there, telling you that you are disturbing their area and should go away as quickly as possible. But if you remain quiet, watching, looking at the beauty of the sunlight among the leaves in the still air, then they will leave you alone, accept you as the squirrels do.

It was not the season, so the cabins were empty and you were alone, and at night it was so silent. And occasionally the bears would come and you could hear their heavy bodies against the cabin. It could have been quite a savage place, for modern civilization had not quite destroyed it. You have to climb from the planes, in and out, up and up and up, until you reach this sequoia forest. There were streams rushing down the slope. It was so extraordinarily beautiful to be alone among these vast,

*In September 1942, Krishnamurti had stayed alone for three weeks in a cabin in the Sequoia National Park where he had been ecstatically happy. It is this experience that he is recalling in his dictation.

very tall great trees, ancient beyond the memory and so utterly unconcerned with what was going on in the world, silent in their ancient dignity and strength. And in this cabin, surrounded by these old ageless trees, you were alone day after day, watching, taking long walks, hardly meeting anyone. From such a height you could see the planes, sunlit, busy; you could see the cars like small insects chasing one another. And up here only the real insects were busy about their day. There were a great many ants. The red ones crawled over your legs but they never seemed to pay much attention to you.

From this cabin you fed the squirrels. There was one particular squirrel that would come every morning and you had a bag of peanuts and you would give them to it one by one: it would stuff it in its mouth, cross over the window-sill and come to the table with its bushy tail curled up, almost touching its head. It would take many of these shelled peanuts, or sometimes even the unshelled ones, and jump back across the window-sill down to the veranda and along the open space into a dead tree with a hollow in it which was its home. It would come perhaps for an hour or more wanting these peanuts, back and forth, back and forth. And it was quite tame by then, you could stroke it, it was so soft, so gentle, it looked with eyes of surprise and then friendship. It knew you wouldn't hurt it. One day, closing all the windows when it was inside and the bag of peanuts was on the table, it took the usual mouthful and then went to the windows and the door, which were all closed, and realized it was a prisoner. It came hopping along to the table, jumped on to it, looked at one and began to scold. After all, you couldn't keep that lively beautiful thing as a prisoner, so you opened the windows. It jumped down to the floor, climbed over the window-sill, went back to the dead trunk and came right back asking for more. From then on we were really great friends. After it had stuffed that hole full of peanuts, probably for the winter, it would go along up the trunks of the trees chasing other squirrels and would always come back to its dead trunk. Then

76

sometimes of an evening it would come to the window-sill and sit there and would chatter, looking at me, telling me something of the day's work, and as it grew darker it said goodnight and jumped back to its home in the hole in the dead old tree. And the next morning early it would be there on the window-sill calling, chattering, and the day would begin.

Every animal in that forest, every little thing, was doing the same — gathering food, chasing others in fun and in anger, and the big animals like the deer were curious and looked at you. And as you climbed to a moderate height and went along a rocky path, you turned and there was a big bear, black with four cubs, as large as large cats. It pushed them up a tree, the four of them, and they climbed up to safety, and then the mother turned round and looked at me. Strangely we weren't afraid. We looked at each other for perhaps two or three seconds or more and then you turned your back and went down the same path. Only then, when you were safe in your cabin, did you realize how dangerous had been this encounter with a mother bear with four cubs.

Life is an endless process of becoming and ending. This great country was still unsophisticated in those days; it was not so terribly advanced technologically and there was not too much vulgarity, as there is now. Sitting on the steps of that cabin you watched and everything was active — the trees, the ants, the rabbits, the deer, the bear and the squirrel. Life is action. Life is a series of continuous, endless action until you die. Action born of desire is distorted, is limited, and this limited action must invariably, do what you will, bring about endless conflict. Anything that is limited must in its very nature breed many problems, crises. It is like a man, like a human being, who is all the time thinking about himself, his problems, his experiences, his joys and pleasures, his business affairs — completely self-centred. The activity of such a person is naturally very limited. One never realizes the limitation of this self-centredness. They call it fulfilment, expressing oneself, achieving success, the

77

pursuit of pleasure and becoming something inwardly, the urge, the desire to be. All such activity must not only be limited and distorted but its successive actions in whatever direction must inevitably breed fragmentation, as is seen in this world. Desire is very strong; the monks and the sannyasis of the world have tried to suppress it, tried to identify that burning flame with some noble symbols or some image — identifying the desire with something greater — but it is still desire. Whatever action comes out of desire, may it be called noble or ignoble, is still limited, distorted.

Now the blue-jay has come back; it is there after its morning meal, scolding to be noticed. And you threw it a few peanuts. It scolded first, then hopped down to the ground, caught a few of them in its beak, flew back on to the branch, flew off, came back scolding. And it too, day by day, became gradually tame. It came quite close with bright eyes, its tail up, the blue shining with such brightness and clarity — a blue that no painter can catch. And it scolded other birds. Probably that was its domain and it didn't want any intruders. But there are always intruders. Other birds soon came. They all seemed to like raisins and peanuts. The whole activity of existence was there.

The sun now was high in the heaven and there were very few shadows, but towards the evening there will be long shadows, shapely, sculptured, dark with a smile.

Is there an action not of desire? If we ask such a question, and we rarely do, one can probe, without any motive, to find an action which is of intelligence. The action of desire is not intelligent; it leads to all kinds of problems and issues. Is there an action of intelligence? One must always be somewhat sceptical in these matters; doubt is an extraordinary factor of purification of the brain, of the heart. Doubt, carefully measured out, brings great clarity, freedom. In the Eastern religions, to doubt, to question, is one of the necessities for finding truth, but in the religious culture of Western civilization, doubt is an abomination of the devil. But in freedom, in an action that is not of desire, there must be the sparkle of doubt. When one actually sees, not theoretically nor verbally, that the action of desire is corrupt, distorted, the very perception is the beginning of that intelligence from which action is totally different. That is, to see the false as the false, the truth in the false, and truth as truth. Such perception is that quality of intelligence which is neither yours nor mine, which then acts. That action has no distortion, no remorse. It doesn't leave a mark, a footprint on the sands of time. That intelligence cannot be unless there is great compassion, love, if you will. There cannot be compassion if the activities of thought are anchored in any one particular ideology or faith, or attached to a symbol or to a person. There must be freedom to be compassionate. And where there is that flame, that very flame is the movement of intelligence.

IT IS ABOUT 1,400 feet up here among the orchards, the orange and avocado, with the hills behind the house. The highest hill around here is about 6,500 feet. Probably it would be called a mountain and the old name is Topa Topa. The former Indians lived here: they must have been very odd and a rather nice race. They may have been cruel but the people who destroyed them were much more cruel. Up here, after a rainy day, nature is waiting breathlessly for another storm, and the world of flowers and the small bushes are rejoicing in this quiet morning, and even the leaves seem so bright, so sharply clear. There is a rose bush that is full of roses, bright red; the beauty of it, the perfume, the stillness of that flower is a marvel.

Going down in the old car which has been kept well polished, the engine running smoothly — going down to the village, through the village, past all those small buildings, schools, and then the open space filled with avocados — going down through the ravine, curving in and out on a smooth road, so well made; then going up and up and up, perhaps over 5,000 feet: there the car stopped and there we were high up, overlooking all the hills which were very green, with bushes, trees and deep ravines. It seemed that we were up among the gods.

Very few used that road, which went on through the desert to a big town miles away, far to your left. As you face the south you see the very far distant sea — the Pacific. It is so very still here. Though man has made this road, fortunately there is no imprint of man. There have been fires up here but that was years ago. You can see some burnt out stumps, black, but round them it has now become green. There have been heavy rains and everything is now in flower, purple, blue and yellow, with here and there

80

bright red spots. The glory of the earth has never been so deeply compassionate as up here.

We sat on the side of the road which was quite clean. It was the earth; earth is always clean. And there were little ants, little insects, crawling, running all over the place. But there are no wild animals up here, which is strange. There may be at night — deer, coyotes and perhaps a few rabbits and hares. Occasionally a car passed by, and that broke the silence, the dignity and the purity of silence. This is really an extraordinary place.

Words cannot measure the expanse, the rolling hills and the vast space, nor the blue sky and the distant desert. It was the whole earth. One hardly dared to talk there was such compelling silence, not to be disturbed. And that silence cannot be measured by words. If you were a poet you would probably measure it with words, put it into a poem, but that which is written is not the actual. The word is not the thing. And here, sitting beside a rock which was becoming warm, man did not exist. The rolling hills, the higher mountains, the great sweeping valleys, deep in blue; there was no you, there was nothing but that.

From ancient times all civilizations have had this concept of measurement. All their marvellous buildings were based on mathematical measurement. When you look at the Acropolis and the glory of the Parthenon, and the hundred and ten floor buildings of New York, they have all had to have this measurement.

Measurement is not only by the rule; measurement exists in the very brain: the tall and the short, the better, the more. This comparative process has existed for time beyond time. We are always comparing. The passing of examinations from school, college, university — our whole way of living has become a series of calculated measurements: the beautiful and the ugly, the noble and ignoble — one's whole set of values, the arguments that end in conclusions, the power of people, the power of nations. Measurement has been necessary to man. And the brain, being conditioned to measurement, to comparison, tries to measure the immeasurable — measuring with words that which cannot ever be measured. It has been a long process for centuries upon centuries — the greater gods and the lesser gods, measuring the vast expanse of the universe and measuring the speed of the athlete. This comparison has brought a great many fears and sorrows.

Now, on that rock, a lizard has come to warm itself quite close to us. You can see its black eyes, its scaly back and the long tail. It is so still, motionless. The sun has made that rock quite warm, and the lizard, coming out of its cold night and warming itself, is waiting for some fly or insect to come along — it will measure the distance and snap it up.

To live without comparison, to live without any kind of measurement inwardly, never to compare what you are with what you should be. The word 'meditation' means not only to ponder, to think over, to probe, to look, to weigh; it also has a much deeper meaning in Sanskrit — to measure, which is 'to become'. In meditation there must be no measurement. This meditation must not be a conscious meditation in deliberately chosen postures. This meditation must be totally unconscious, never knowing that *you* are meditating. If you deliberately meditate it is another form of desire, as any other expression of desire. The objects may vary; your meditation may be to reach the highest, but the motive is the desire to achieve, as the business man, as the builder of a great cathedral. Meditation is a movement without any motive, without words and the activity of thought. It must be something that is not deliberately set about. Only then is meditation a movement in the infinite, measureless to man, without a goal, without an end and without a beginning. And that has a strange action in daily life, because all life is one and then becomes sacred. And that which is sacred can never be killed. To kill another is unholy. It cries to heaven as a bird kept in a cage. One never realizes how sacred life is, not only your little life but the lives of millions of others, from the things of nature to extraordinary human beings. And in meditation which is without measurement, there is the very action of that which is most noble, most sacred and holy.

The other day on the banks of a river* — how lovely are rivers; there isn't only one sacred river, all rivers throughout the world have their own divinity — the other day a man was sitting on the banks of a river wrapt in a fawn coloured cloth. His hands were hidden, his eyes were shut and his body was very still. He had beads in his hands and he was repeating some words and the hands were moving from bead to bead. He had done this for many years and he never missed a bead. And the river rolled along beside him. Its current was deep. It began among the great mountains, snow-clad and distant; it began as a small stream, and as it moved south it gathered all the small streams and rivers and became a great river. In that part of the world they worshipped it. One does not know for how many years this man had been repeating his mantra and rolling the beads. He was meditating — at least people thought he was meditating and probably he did too. So all the passers-by looked at him, became silent and then went on with their laughter and chatter. That almost motionless figure — one could see through the cloth only a slight action of the fingers — had sat there for a very long time, completely absorbed, for he heard no other sound than the sound of his own words and the rhythm of it, the music of it. And he would say that he was meditating. There are a thousand others like him, all over the world, in quiet deep monasteries among the hills and towns and beside the rivers.

Meditation is not words, a mantram, or self-hypnosis, the drug of illusions. It must happen without your volition. It must take place in the quiet stillness of the night, when you are suddenly awake and see that the brain is quiet and there is a peculiar quality of meditation going on. It must take place as silently as a

*This is a memory from when he was at Benares on the banks of the Ganges.

snake among the tall grass, green in the fresh morning light. It must take place in the deep recesses of the brain. Meditation is not an achievement. There is no method, system or practice. Meditation begins with the ending of comparison, the ending of the becoming or not becoming. As the bee whispers among the leaves so the whispering of meditation is action.

THE CLOUDS ARE still hanging over the hills, the valley and the mountains. Occasionally there is an opening in the sky and the sun comes through, bright, clear, but soon it disappears. One likes this kind of morning, cool, fresh, with the whole world green around you. As the summer comes on the sun will burn all the green grass, and the meadows across the valley will be parched, dry, and all the grass with the bright green will have gone. In the summer all the freshness has gone.

One likes these quiet mornings. The oranges are so bright and the leaves, dark green, are shining. And there is a perfume in the air from the orange blossom, strong, almost suffocating. There is a different kind of orange to be picked later on before the summer heat. Now there is the green leaf, the orange and the flower on the same tree at the same time. It is a beautiful world and man is so indifferent to it, spoiling the earth, the rivers and the bays and the fresh-water lakes.

But let's leave all that behind and walk along a narrow path, up the hill where there is a little stream which in a few weeks will be dry. You and a friend are walking along the path, talking now and then, looking at all the various colours of green. What a variety there is, from the lightest green, the Nile green, and perhaps even lighter, bluer, to the dark greens, luscious, full of their own richness. And as you go along up the path, just managing to walk along together side by side, you happen to pick up something ravishingly beautiful, sparkling, a jewel of extra-ordinary antiquity and beauty. You are so astonished to find it on this path of so many animals which only a few people have trodden. You look at it with great astonishment. It is so subtly made, so intricate that no jeweller's hand can ever have made it.

85

You hold it for some time, amazed and silent. Then you put it very carefully in your inside pocket, button it, and are almost frightened that you might lose it or that it might lose its sparkling, shining beauty. And you put your hand outside the pocket that holds it. The other sees you doing this and sees that your face and your eyes have undergone a remarkable change. There is a kind of ecstasy, a speechless wonder, a breathless excitement.

When the man asks: 'What is it that you have found and are so extraordinarily elated by?' you reply in a very soft, gentle voice (it seems so strange to you to hear your own voice) that you picked up truth. You don't want to talk about it, you are rather shy; the very talking might destroy it. And the man who is walking beside you is slightly annoyed that you are not communicating with him freely, and he says that if you have found the truth, then let's go down into the valley and organize it so that others will understand it, so that others will grasp it and perhaps it will help them. You don't reply, you are sorry that you ever told him about it.

The trees are full of bloom. Even up here on the slight breeze coming up the valley you smell the orange blossom and look down the valley and see the many orange trees and feel the quiet, still, breathless air. But you have come upon something that is most precious, that can never be told to another. They may find it, but you have it, grasp it and adore it.

Institutions and organizations throughout the world have not helped man. There are all the physical organizations for one's needs; the institutions of war, of democracy, the institutions of tyranny and the institutions of religion — they have had their day and they continue, and man looks up to them, longing to be helped, not only physically but inside the skin, inside the throbbing ache, the shadow of time and the far reaching thoughts. There have been institutions of many, many kinds from the most ancient of days, and they have not inwardly

changed man. Institutions can never change man psychologically, deeply. And one wonders why man created them, for all the
institutions in the world are put together by man, hoping that
they might help him, that they might give him some kind of
lasting security. And strangely they have not. We never seem to
realize this fact. We are creating more and more institutions,
more and more organizations — one organization opposing
another.

Thought is inventing all these, not only the democratic
organizations or the totalitarian organizations; thought is also
perceiving, realizing, that what it has created has not basically
changed the structure, the nature of one's own self. The
institutions, the organizations and all religions are put together
by thought, by cunning, clever, erudite thought. What thought
has created, brought about, shapes its own thinking. And one
asks oneself, if one is serious, earnest in one's enquiry: why has
not thought realized its own activity? Can thought be aware of its
own movement? Can thought see itself, see what it is doing, both
in the outer and the inner?

There is really no outer and inner: the inner creates the outer,
and the outer then shapes the inner. This ebb and flow of action
and reaction is the movement of thought, and thought is always
trying to overcome the outer, and succeeds, bringing about many
problems; in solving one problem other problems arise. Thought
has also shaped the inner, moulded it according to the outer
demands. This seemingly endless process has created this
society, ugly, cruel, immoral and violent. And having created it,
the inner becomes a slave to it. The outer shapes the inner and
the inner shapes the outer. This process has been going on for
thousands upon thousands of years and thought seems not to
realize its own activity. So one asks: can thought ever be aware of
itself — aware of what it is doing? There is no thinker apart from
thought; thought has made the thinker, the experiencer, the
analyser. The thinker, the one who is watching, the one who acts,
is the past, with all the inheritance of man, genetically, biologic-

ally — the traditions, the habits and all accumulated knowledge. After all, the past is knowledge, and the thinker is not separate from the past. Thought has created the past, thought *is* the past; then thought divides the thinker and the thought, which the thinker must shape, control. But that is a fallacy; there is only thought. The self *is* the 'me', the past. Imagination may project the future but it is still the activity of thought.

So thought, which is the outcome of knowledge, has not changed man and will never change him because knowledge is always limited and will always be limited. So again one asks: can thought become aware of itself, thought which has put together all our consciousness — action and reaction, the sensory response, the sensuality, the fears, the aspirations, the pursuit of pleasure, all the agony of loneliness and the suffering which man has brought upon himself through wars, through his irresponsibility, through callous self-centredness? All that is the activity of thought, which has invented the limitless and the god who lives in the limitless. All that is the activity of time and thought.

When one comes to this point one asks the old instrument, which is worn out, whether it can bring about a radical mutation in man, which is, after all, the brain. When thought realizes itself, sees where knowledge is necessary in the physical world and realizes its own limitation, it then becomes quiet, silent. Only then is there a new instrument which is not put together by time or thought, totally unrelated to knowledge. It is this instrument — perhaps the word instrument may be wrong — it is this perception which is always fresh, because it has no past, no remembrance; it is intelligence born of compassion. That perception brings a deep mutation in the very brain cells themselves, and its action is always the right action, clear, precise, without the shadow of the past and time.

IT IS A spring morning, a morning that has never been before and never will be again.

It is a spring morning. Every little blade of grass, the camelias, the roses, all are blooming and there is perfume in the air.

It is a spring morning and the earth is so alive, and up in this valley all the mountains are green and the tallest of them so extraordinarily vital, immovable and majestic. It is a morning that as you go along the path and look around at the beauty and the ground squirrels, every tender leaf of the spring is shining in the sun. Those leaves have been waiting for this the whole winter and have just come out, tender, vulnerable. And without being romantic, imaginative, there is a feeling of great love and compassion, for there is so much beauty, incorruptible. There have been a thousand spring mornings but never such a morning as this, so still, so quiet, breathless — perhaps it is with adoration. And the squirrels are out and so are the lizards.

It is a spring morning and the air is festive; there are festivals all over the world because it is spring. The festivals are expressed in so many different ways but that which *is* can never be expressed in words. Everywhere, with the song and the dance, there is a deep feeling of spring.

Why is it that we seem to be losing the highly vulnerable quality of sensitivity — sensitivity to all the things about us, not only to our own problems and turmoils? To be actually sensitive, not about something but just to be sensitive, to be vulnerable, like that new leaf, which was born a few days ago to face storms, rain, darkness and light. When we are vulnerable we seem to get hurt; being hurt we withdraw into ourselves, build a wall around ourselves, become hard, cruel. But when we are vulnerable

89

without any ugly, brutal reactions, vulnerable to all the movements of one's own being, vulnerable to the world, so sensitive that there is no regret, no wounds, no self-imposed discipline, then there is the quality of measureless existence.

We lose all this vulnerability in the world of noise and brutality, vulgarity and the bustle of everyday life. To have one's senses sharpened, not any one particular sense but to have all the senses fully awake, which does not necessarily mean to indulge — to be sensitive to all the movements of thought, the feelings, the pains, the loneliness, the anxiety — with those senses fully awakened, there is a different kind of sensation that goes beyond all the sensory or sensual responses. Have you ever looked at the sea, or at those vast mountains, the Himalayas, which stretch from horizon to horizon — have you ever watched a flower, with all your senses? When there is such observation there is no centre from which you are observing, there is no 'me'. The 'me', the limited observation of one or two senses, breeds the egotistic movement. After all, we live by the senses, by sensation, and it is only when thought creates the image out of the sensations that all the complexities of desire arise.

On this morning, you look down into the valley, seeing the extraordinary spread of green and the distant town, feeling the pure air, watching all the crawling things of the earth, watching without the interference of the images thought has built. Now the breeze is blowing from the valley up the canyon and you turn as the path turns. Going down, there is a bob cat right in front of you, about ten feet away. You can hear it purring, rubbing itself against a rock, the hair sticking out of its ears, its short tail and extraordinary, graceful movement. It is a spring morning for it too. We walked together down the path and it was hardly making any noise except for its purring, highly enjoying itself, delighted to be out in the spring sunshine; it was so clean that its hair was sparkling. And as you watch it, the whole wild nature is in that animal. You tread on a dead branch which makes a noise, and it is off, not even looking behind it; that noise indicated man, the most dangerous of all animals. It is gone in a second among bushes and rocks and all the joy has gone out of it. It knows how cruel man is and it doesn't want to wait; it wants to be away, as far away as possible.

It is a spring morning and it is peaceful. Aware that a man was behind it, a few feet away, that cat must have instinctively responded to the image of what man is — the man who has killed so many things, destroyed so many cities, destroyed culture after culture, ever pursuing his desires, always seeking some kind of security and pleasure.

Desire, which has been the driving force in man, has created a great many pleasant and useful things; desire also, in man's relationships, has created a great many problems and turmoils and misery — the desire for pleasure. The monks and the sannyasis of the world have tried to go beyond it, have forced themselves to worship an ideal, an image, a symbol. But desire is always there like a flame, burning. And to find out, to probe into the nature of desire, the complexity of desire, its activities, its demands, its fulfilments — ever more and more desire for power, position, prestige, status, the desire for the unnameable, that which is beyond all our daily life — has made man do all kinds of ugly and brutal things. Desire is the outcome of sensation — the outcome with all the images that thought has built. And this desire not only breeds discontent but a sense of hopelessness. Never suppress it, never discipline it but probe into the nature of it — what is the origin, the purpose, the intricacies of it? To delve deep into it is not another desire, for it has no motive; it is like understanding the beauty of a flower, to sit down beside it and look at it. And as you look it begins to reveal itself as it actually is — the extraordinarily delicate colour, the perfume, the petals, the stem and the earth out of which it has grown. So look at this desire and its nature without thought which is always shaping sensations, pleasure and pain, reward and punishment. Then one understands, not verbally, nor intellectually, the whole causation of desire, the root of desire. The very perception of it, the subtle perception of it, that in itself is intelligence. And that intelligence will always act sanely and rationally in dealing with desire.

So without too much talk this morning, without too much thinking, to be entirely enveloped by this spring morning, to live with it, to walk in it, is a joy that is beyond all measure. It cannot be repeated. It will be there until there is a knock on the door.

ONE SAW A bird dying, shot by a man. It was flying with rhythmic beat and beautifully, with such freedom and lack of fear. And the gun shattered it; it fell to the earth and all the life had gone out of it. A dog fetched it, and the man collected other dead birds. He was chattering with his friend and seemed so utterly indifferent. All that he was concerned with was bringing down so many birds, and it was over as far as he was concerned. They are killing all over the world. Those marvellous, great animals of the sea, the whales, are killed by the million, and the tiger and so many other animals are now becoming endangered species. Man is the only animal that is to be dreaded.

Some time ago, staying with a friend high in the hills, a man came and told the host that a tiger had killed a cow last night, and would we like to see the tiger that evening? He could arrange it by building a platform in a tree and tying up a goat, and the bleat of the goat, of the small animal, would attract the tiger and we could see it. We both refused to satisfy our curiosity so cruelly. But later that day the host suggested that we get the car and go into the forest to see the tiger if we could. So towards evening we got into an open car with a chauffeur driving us and went deep into the forest for several miles. Of course we saw nothing. It was getting quite dark and the headlights were on, and as we turned round, there it was sitting right in the middle of the road waiting to receive us. It was a very large animal, beautifully marked, and its eyes, caught by the headlights, were bright, scintillating. It came growling towards the car, and as it passed just a few inches from the hand that was stretched out, the host said, 'Don't touch it, it is too dangerous, be quick for it is faster than your hand.' But you could feel the energy of that animal, its vitality; it was a great dynamo of energy. And as it passed by one felt an enormous attraction towards it. And it disappeared into the woods.*

Apparently the friend had seen many tigers and had helped long ago in his youth to kill one, and ever since he had been regretting the terrible act. Cruelty in every form is now spreading in the world. Man has probably never been so cruel as he is now, so violent. The churches and the priests of the world have talked about peace on earth; from the highest Christian hierarchy to the poor village priest there has been talk about living a good life, not hurting, not killing a thing; especially the Buddhists and Hindus of former years have said, 'Don't kill the fly, don't kill anything, for next life you will pay for it.' That was rather crudely put but some of them maintained this spirit, this intention not to kill and not to hurt another human being. But killing with wars is going on and on. The dog so quickly kills the rabbit. Or the man shoots another with his marvellous machines, and he himself is perhaps shot by another. And this killing has been going on for millenia upon millenia. Some treat it as a sport, others kill out of hatred, anger, jealousy, and organized murder by the various nations with their armaments goes on. One wonders if man will ever live on this beautiful earth peacefully, never killing a little thing, or being killed, or killing another, but live peacefully with some divinity and love in his heart.

In this part of the world, which we call the West, the Christians have perhaps killed more than anyone else. They are always talking about peace on this earth. But to have peace one must live peacefully, and that seems so utterly impossible. There are arguments for and against war, the arguments that man has always been a killer and will always remain so, and those who maintain that he can bring about a change in himself and not kill. This is a very old story. The endless butchering has become a habit, an accepted formula, in spite of all the religions.

One was watching the other day a red-tailed hawk, high in the

*Krishnamurti tells of this meeting with a tiger more fully in his *Journal*, p. 40.

94

heavens, circling effortlessly, without a beat of the wing, just for the fun of flying, just to be sustained by the air-currents. Then it was joined by another, and they were flying together for quite a while. They were marvellous creatures in that blue sky, and to hurt them in any way is a crime against heaven. Of course there is no heaven; man has invented heaven out of hope, for his life has become a hell, an endless conflict from birth to death, coming and going, making money, working endlessly. This life has become a turmoil, a travail of endless striving. One wonders if man, a human being, will ever live on this earth peacefully. Conflict has been the way of his life — within the skin and outside the skin, in the area of the psyche and in the society which that psyche has created.

Probably love has totally disappeared from this world. Love implies generosity, care, not to hurt another, not to make another feel guilty, to be generous, courteous, and behave in such a manner that your words and thoughts are born out of compassion. Of course you cannot be compassionate if you belong to organized religious institutions — large, powerful, traditional, dogmatic, that insist on faith. There must be freedom to love. That love is not pleasure, desire, a remembrance of things that have gone. Love is not the opposite of jealousy, hate and anger.

All this may sound rather Utopian, idealistic; something that man can only aspire to. But if you believe that then you will go on killing. Love is as real, as strong, as death. It has nothing to do with imagination, or sentiment, or romanticism; and naturally it has nothing to do with power, position, prestige. It is as still as the waters of the sea and as powerful as the sea; it is like the running waters of a rich river flowing endlessly, without a beginning or an end. But the man who kills the baby seals, or the great whales, is concerned with his livelihood. He would say, 'I live by that, that is my trade.' He is totally unconcerned with that something which we call love. He probably loves his family — or he thinks he loves his family — and he is not very much concerned with how he gains his livelihood. Perhaps that is one of the reasons why man lives a fragmentary life; he never seems to love what he is doing — though perhaps a few people do. If one lived by the work one loves, it would be very different — one would understand the wholeness of life. We have broken up life into fragments: the business world, the artistic world, the scientific world, the political world and the religious world. We seem to think that they are all separate and should be kept separate. So we become hypocritical, doing something ugly, corrupt, in the business world and then coming home to live peacefully with our family; this breeds hypocrisy, a double standard of life.

It is really a marvellous earth. That bird sitting on the tallest tree has been sitting there every morning, looking over the world, watching for a greater bird, a bird that might kill it, watching the clouds, the passing shadow, and the great spread of this rich earth, these rivers, forests and all the men who work from morning until night. If one thinks at all, in the psychological world, it is to be full of sorrow. One wonders too if man will ever change, or only the few, the very, very few. Then what is the relationship of the few to the many? Or, what is the relationship of the many to the few? The many have no relationship to the few. The few do have a relationship.

Sitting on that rock, looking down into the valley, with a lizard beside you, you daren't move in case the lizard should be disturbed or frightened. And the lizard too is watching. And so the world goes on: inventing gods, following the hierarchy of god's representatives; and all the sham and the shame of illusions will probably go on, the thousand problems getting more and more complex and intricate. Only the intelligence of love and compassion can solve all problems of life. That intelligence is the only instrument that can never become dull, useless.

IT IS A foggy morning, you can hardly see the orange trees which are about ten feet away. It is cold and all the hills and the mountains are hidden, and there is dew on the leaves. It will clear up later. It is early morning yet and the beautiful Californian sun and cool breeze will come a little later on.

One wonders why human beings have always been so cruel, so ugly in their responses to any statement they don't like, aggressive, ready to attack. This has been going on for thousands of years. One hardly ever meets nowadays a gentle person who is ready to yield, totally generous and happy in his relationships.

Last night there was the hooting of the owl; it was a great-horned owl, it must be very large. And it waited for its mate to reply, and the mate replied from a distance and the hoot went down into the valley and you could hardly hear it. It was such a perfectly still night, dark, and strangely quiet.

Everything seems to live in order, in its own order — the sea with its tides, the new moon and the setting of the full moon, the lovely spring and the warmth of summer. Even the earthquake of yesterday has its own order. Order is the very essence of the universe — the order of birth and death and so on. It is only man that seems to live in such disorder, confusion. He has lived that way since the owl began.

Talking to the visitor sitting on the veranda, with the red climbing rose and a young wisteria and the smell of the earth and the trees, it seemed such a pity to discuss disorder. When you look around at those dark hills and the rocky mountain and hear the whisper of a stream which will soon be dry in summer, it all

*Between April 26 and May 1 Krishnamurti had been to San Francisco and given two talks in the Masonic Hall and a radio interview.

has such curious order that to discuss human disorder, human confusion and misery, seems so utterly out of place. But there he is, friendly, knowledgeable and probably given to thought.

The mocking bird is on the telephone wire; it is doing what it generally does — flying into the air, circling and landing on the wire and then mocking at the world. This it does so often and the world apparently doesn't care. But the bird still mocks on.

The fog is clearing, there is that spring sunshine and the lizard is coming out, warming itself on the rock, and all the little things of the earth are busy. They have their order, they have their pleasure, amusement. They all seem to be so happy, enjoying the sunshine, no man near to hurt them, to spoil their day.

'If one may ask,' the visitor began, 'what to you is the most important thing in life? What to you is the most essential quality that man must cultivate?'

'If you cultivate, as you cultivate the fields of the earth, then it is not the most essential thing. It must happen naturally — whatever happens — naturally, easily, without any self-centred motives. The most important thing for each human being, surely, is to live in order, in harmony with all the things around him — even with the noise of the great towns, even with something that is ugly, vulgar, without letting it affect or alter the course of his life, alter or distort the order in which he is living. Surely, sir, order is the most important thing in life, or, rather, one of the most important.'

'Why,' he asks, 'should order be a quality of a brain that can act correctly, happily, precisely?'

'Order isn't created by thought. Order isn't something that you follow day after day, practise, conform to. As the streams join the sea, so the stream of order, the river of order, is endless. But that order cannot be if there is any kind of effort, any kind of struggle to achieve, or to put aside disorder and slip into a routine, into various well defined habits. All that is not order. Conflict is the very source of disorder, is the very cause.'

'Everything struggles, doesn't it? Those trees, they have struggled to exist, struggled to grow. The marvellous oak there behind this house, it has withstood storms, years of rain and hot sunshine, it has struggled to exist. Life is conflict, it is a turmoil, a storm. And you are saying, are you not, that order is a state in which there is no conflict? It seems almost impossible, like talking in a strange language, something utterly foreign to one's own life, one's own way of thinking. Do you, if I am not impudent, live in order in which there is no conflict whatsoever?'

'Is it very important, sir, to find out if another is living without effort, without conflict? Or would you rather ask if you, as a human being, who live in disorder, can find out for yourself the many causes — or perhaps there is only one cause — of this disorder? Those flowers know neither order nor disorder, they just exist. Of course, if they were not watered, looked after, they would die, and dying also is their order. The bright, hot sun will destroy them next month, and to them that is order.'

The lizard has warmed itself on the rock and is waiting for the flies to come. And surely they will come. And the lizard with its quick tongue will swallow them. It seems to be the nature of the world: the big things live on little things, and the bigger live on the big. This is the cycle in the world of nature. And in that there is neither order nor disorder. But we know for ourselves from time to time the sense of total harmony and also the pain, the anxiety, the sorrow, the conflict. The cause of disorder is the everlasting becoming — to become, to seek identity, the struggle to be. As long as the brain, which is so heavily conditioned, is measuring, 'the more', 'the better', moving psychologically from this to that, it must inevitably bring about a sense of conflict, and this is disorder. Not only the words, 'more', 'better', but the feeling, the reaction of achieving, gaining — as long as there is this division, duality, there must be conflict. And out of conflict is disorder.

Perhaps one is aware of all this, but being negligent of this awareness, one carries on in the same way day after day all the days of one's life. This duality is not only verbal but has the deeper division as the thinker and the thought, as the thinker separate from himself. The thinker is put together by thought, the thinker is the past, the thinker is knowledge, and thought too is born out of knowledge. Actually there is no division between the thinker and the thought, they are one inseparable unit; but thought plays a clever trick upon itself, it divides itself. Perhaps this constant division of itself, its own fragmentation, is the cause of disorder. Just to see, to realize, the truth of this, that the perceiver is the perceived, ends disorder.

The mocking bird has gone and the mourning dove is there with its plaintive cry. And soon its mate joins it. They sit together on that wire, silent, motionless, but their eyes are moving, looking, watching for danger. The red-tailed hawk and the predatory birds who were there an hour or two ago have gone. Perhaps they will come back tomorrow. And so the morning ends and the sun now is bright and there are a thousand shadows. The earth is quiet and man is lost and confused.

IT WAS A pleasant morning, cloudy, a slight nip in the air, and the hills were covered and quiet. There was a scent of orange blossom, not very strong but it was there. It is a peculiar, penetrating smell and it came into the room. And all the flowers this morning were ready for the sun to come out. The clouds would soon pass away and there would be bright sunshine later on.

The car went through the little village, past the many small hamlets, the oil derricks, oil tanks, and all the activity around those oil fields, and at last you came to the sea. You passed again through a big town, not too big, past the various lemon and orange groves, and you came upon, not patches of strawberries, not small cabbage fields, but acres of them, miles of them — strawberries, celery, spinach, lettuce and other vegetables — miles of flat rich soil between the hills and the sea. Here everything is done on a grand scale, almost too extravagant — miles of lemons and oranges, walnuts and so on. It is a rich land, beautiful. And the hills were so friendly that morning.

At last you came to the blue Pacific. It was like a pond this morning, so quiet, so extraordinarily still, and the morning light was on it. One should really meditate on that light, not directly on the sun but on the reflection of the sun on the glittering water. But the sea is not always like that; a month or two ago it rolled in fury, smashing the pier, destroying the houses around the beach, bringing havoc, even to the high road along it. Now they were repairing the smashed pier with all the lumber washed ashore, great quantities of it. Today, though, like a tamed animal, you could stroke it, you could feel the depth and the width and the beauty of this vast sea, so blue. Nearer the shore it was a Nile

101

green. To go along that road beside the sea in the salty air was a most pleasant thing, just to see the hills, the waving grass and the vast sea of water.

All this disappeared into the huge ugly town, a city that has spread for miles upon miles upon miles. It was not a very pleasant city, but people lived there and seemed to like it.

I don't know if, sitting on the beach, you have ever watched the sea, watched the waves come and go. The seventh wave seems to be the largest, thundering towards the land. There is very little tide in the Pacific — at least not here, not like those tides that pull out many miles and come in so rapidly. Here there is always a little ebb and flow, coming in and going out, repeated for centuries upon centuries. If you can look at that sea, the sparkle of the dazzling light, and the clear water, with all your senses highly awakened to their excellence, in that observation there is not the centre, as you, watching. It is a beautiful thing to watch that sea, and the sand, clean, washed every day. No footprint can remain there, even the little birds of the sea never leave their mark, the sea washes them away.

The houses along the beach are small, tidy; probably very rich people live along there. But all that doesn't count for anything — their riches, their vulgarity, their smart cars. One saw a very old Mercedes with exhaust pipes outside the bonnet, three on each side. The owners seemed to be very proud of it, they had polished it, washed it, taken such great care of it. Probably they had bought that machine rather than many other things. You could still do a great many miles in it; it was well put together to last.

Sitting on the shore watching the birds, the sky, and hearing the distant sound of passing cars, it was a most beautiful morning. You went out with the ebb and came in with the tide. You went out far and came back again — this endless movement of in and out and out and in. You could see as far as the horizon where the sky met the waters. It was a big bay with blue and white water and tiny little houses all around it. And behind you were

102

the mountains, range after range. Watching without a single thought, watching without any reaction, watching without identity, only endlessly watching, you really are not awake, you are absent minded, not all there; you are not you but watching. Watching the thoughts that arise and then fade away, thought after thought, thought itself is becoming aware of itself. There is no thinker watching the thought, the thinker is the thought.

Sitting on the beach watching the people pass by, two or three couples and a single woman, it seems that all nature, everything around you, from the deep blue sea to those high rocky mountains, was also watching. We are watching, not waiting, not expecting anything to happen but watching without end. In that watching there is learning, not the accumulation of knowledge through learning that is almost mechanical, but watching closely, never superficially but deeply, with a swiftness and a tenderness; then there is no watcher. When there is a watcher it is merely the past watching, and that is not watching, that is just remembering and it is rather dead stuff. Watching is tremendously alive, every moment a vacancy. Those little crabs and those seagulls and all those birds flying by are watching. They are watching for prey, for fish, watching for something to eat; they too are watching. Somebody passes close by you and wonders what you are watching. You are watching nothing, and in that nothingness everything is.

The other day a man who had travelled a great deal, seen a great deal, written something or other, came — an oldish man with a beard, which was well kept; he was dressed decently without the sloppiness of vulgarity. He took care of his shoes, of his clothes. He spoke excellent English, though he was a foreigner. And to the man who was sitting on the beach watching, he said he had talked to a great many people, discussed with some professors and scholars, and while he was in India he had talked to some of the pundits. And most of them, it seemed, according to him, were not concerned with society, not deeply committed to any social reform or to the present crisis of war. He was deeply concerned about the society in which we were living, though he was not a social reformer. He was not quite sure whether society could be changed, whether you could do something about it. But he saw what it was; the vast corruption, the absurdity of the politicians, the pettiness, the vanity, and the brutality that is rampant in the world.

He said, 'What can we do about this society? — not petty little reforms here and there, changing one President for another, or one Prime Minister for another — they are all of the same breed more or less; they can't do much because they represent the mediocrity, or even less than that, the vulgarity; they want to show off, they will never do anything. They will bring about potty little reforms here and there but society will go on in spite of them.' He had watched the various societies, cultures. They are not so very different fundamentally. He appeared to be a very serious man with a smile and he talked about the beauty of this country, the vastness, the variety, from the hot deserts to the high Rockies with their splendour. One listened to him as one would listen to and watch the sea.

Society cannot be changed unless man changes. Man, you and others, have created these societies for generations upon generations; we have all created these societies out of our pettiness, narrowness, out of our limitation, out of our greed, envy, brutality, violence, competition, and so on. We are responsible for the mediocrity, the stupidity, the vulgarity, for all the tribal nonsense and religious sectarianism. Unless each one of us changes radically, society will never change. It is there, we have made it, and then it makes us. It shapes us, as we have shaped it. It puts us in a mould and the mould puts it into a framework which is the society.

So this action is going on endlessly, like the sea with a tide that goes far out and then comes in, sometimes very, very slowly, at other times rapidly, dangerously. In and out; action, reaction, action. This seems to be the nature of this movement, unless there is deep order in oneself. That very order will bring about order in society, not through legislation, governments and all that business—though as long as there is disorder, confusion, the law, the authority, which is created by our disorder, will go on. Law is the making of man, as the society is — the product of man is law.

So the inner, the psyche, creates the outer according to its limitation; and the outer then controls and moulds the inner. The Communists have thought, and probably still do, that by controlling the outer, bringing about certain laws, regulations, institutions, certain forms of tyranny, they can change man. But so far they have not succeeded, and they never will succeed. This is also the activity of the Socialists. The Capitalists do it in a different way, but it is the same thing. The inner always overcomes the outer, for the inner is far more strong, far more vital, than the outer.

Can this movement ever stop — the inner creating the outer environment psychologically, and the outer, the law, the institutions, the organizations, trying to shape man, the brain, to act in a certain way, and the brain, the inner, the psyche, then changing, circumventing the outer? This movement has been going on as long as man has been on this earth, crudely, superficially, sometimes brilliantly — it is always the inner overcoming the outer, like the sea with its tides going out and coming in. One should really ask whether this movement can ever stop—action and reaction, hatred and more hatred, violence and more violence. It has an end when there is only watching, without motive, without response, without direction. Direction comes into being when there is accumulation. But watching, in which there is attention, awareness, and a great sense of compassion, has its own intelligence. This watching and intelligence act. And that action is not the ebb and flow. But this requires great alertness, to see things without the word, without the name, without any reaction; in that watching there is a great vitality, passion.

YOU WERE ALREADY fairly high up, looking down into the valley, and if you climb a mile or more up and up the winding path, passing all kinds of vegetation — live oaks, sage, poison oak — and past a stream which is always dry in the summer, you can see the blue sea far away in the distance, across range after range. Up here it is absolutely quiet. It is so still there isn't a breath of air. You look down and the mountains look down on you. You can go on climbing up the mountain for many hours, down into another valley and up again. You have done it several times before, twice reaching the very top of those rocky mountains. Beyond them to the north is a vast plain of desert. Down there it is very hot, here it is quite cold; you have to put something on in spite of the hot sun.

And as you come down, looking at the various trees, plants and little insects, suddenly you hear the rattle of a rattle snake. And you jump, fortunately away from the rattler. You are only about ten feet away from it. It is still rattling. You look at each other and watch. Snakes have no eyelids. This one was not very long but quite thick, as thick as your arm. You keep your distance and you watch it very carefully, its pattern, its triangular head and its black tongue flickering in and out. You watch each other. It doesn't move and you don't move. But presently, its head and its tail towards you, it slithers back and you step forward. Again its coils up and rattles and you watch each other. And again, with its head and tail towards you, it begins to go back and again you move forward; and again it coils and rattles. You do this for several minutes, perhaps ten minutes or more; then it gets tired. You see that it is motionless, waiting, but as you approach it, it doesn't rattle. It has temporarily lost its energy.

106

You are quite close to it. Unlike the cobra which stands up to strike, this snake strikes lunging forward. But there was no movement. It was too exhausted, so you leave it. It was really quite a poisonous, dangerous thing. Probably you could touch it but you are disinclined to, though not frightened. You feel that you would rather not touch it and you leave it alone.

And as you come further down you almost step on a quail with about a dozen or more babies. They scatter into the nearby bushes, and the mother too disappears into a bush and they all call to each other. You go down and wait, and if you have the patience to watch, you presently see them all come together under the mother's wing. It is cool up there and they are waiting for the sun to warm the air and the earth.

You come down across the little stream, past a meadow which is almost losing its green, and return to your room rather tired but exhilarated by the walk and by the morning sun. You see the orange trees with their bright yellow oranges, the rose bushes and the myrtle, and the tall eucalyptus trees. It is all very peaceful in the house.

It was a pleasant morning, full of strange activities on the earth. All those little things alive, rushing about, seeking their morning food — the squirrel, the gopher. They eat the tender roots of plants and are quite destructive. A dog can kill them so quickly with a snap. It is very dry, the rains are over and gone, to return again perhaps in four months or more. All the valley below is still glistening. It is strange how there is a brooding silence over the whole earth. In spite of the noise of towns and the traffic, there is something almost palpable, something holy. If you are in harmony with nature, with all the things around you, then you are in harmony with all human beings. If you have lost your relationship with nature you will inevitably lose your relationship with human beings.

A whole group of us sitting at table towards the end of the meal began a serious conversation as has happened several times before. It was about the meaning of words, the weight of the word, the content of the word, not merely the superficial meaning of the word but the depth of it, the quality of it, the feeling of it. Of course the word is never the actual thing. The description, the explanation, is not that which is described, nor that about which there is an explanation. The word, the phrase, the explanation are not the actuality. But the word is used as a communication of one's thought, one's feeling, and the word, though it is not communicated to another, holds the feeling inside oneself. The actual never conditions the brain, but the theory, the conclusion, the description, the abstraction, do condition it. The table never conditions the brain but god does, whether it is the god of the Hindus, Christians or Muslims. The concept, the image, conditions the brain, not that which is actually happening, taking place.

To the Christian, the word Jesus or Christ has great significance, great meaning, it evokes a deep sentiment, a sensation. Those words have no meaning to the Hindu, to the Buddhist, or to the Muslim. Those words are not the actual. So those words, which have been used for two thousand years, have conditioned the brain. The Hindu has his own gods, his own divinities. Those divinities, as the Christians', are the projections of thought, out of fear, out of pleasure and so on.

It seems that language really doesn't condition the brain; what does is the theory of the language, the abstraction of a certain feeling and the abstraction taking the form of an idea, a symbol, a person — not the actual person but a person imagined, or hoped for, or projected by thought. All those abstractions, those ideas, conclusions, however strong, condition the brain. But the actual, like the table, never does.

Take a word like 'suffering'. That word has a different meaning for the Hindu and the Christian. But suffering, however described by words, is shared by all of us. Suffering is the fact, the actual. But when we try to escape from it through some theory, or through some idealized person, or through a symbol, those

108

forms of escape mould the brain. Suffering as a fact doesn't and this is important to realize.

Like the word 'attachment'; to see the word, to hold it as if in your hand and watch it, feel the depth of it, the whole content of it, the consequences of it, the fact that we are attached — the fact, not the word; that feeling doesn't shape the brain, put it into a mould, but the moment one moves away from it, that is, when thought moves away from the fact, that very movement away, movement of escape, is not only a time factor, but the beginning of shaping the brain in a certain mould.

To the Buddhist the word Buddha, the impression, the image, creates great reverence, great feeling, devotion; he seeks refuge in the image which thought has created. And as the thought is limited, because all knowledge is always limited, that very image brings about conflict — the feeling of reverence to a person, or to a symbol, or to a certain long-established tradition — but the *feeling* of reverence itself, divorced from all the external images, symbols and so on, is not a factor of conditioning the brain.

There, sitting in the next chair, was a modified Christian. And when across the table one mentioned Christ one could immediately feel the restrictive, reverential reserve. That word has conditioned the brain. It is quite extraordinary to watch this whole phenomenon of communication with words, each race giving different significance and meaning to the word and thereby creating a division, a limitation, to the feeling which mankind suffers. The suffering of mankind is common, is shared by all human beings. The Russian may express it in one way, the Hindu, the Christian in another and so on, but the fact of suffering, the actual feeling of pain, grief, loneliness, that feeling never shapes or conditions the brain. So one becomes very attentive to, aware of, the subtleties of the word, the meaning, the weight of it.

The universal, the global feeling of all human beings and their inter-relationship, can only come into being when the words 'nation', 'tribe', 'religion', have all disappeared. Either the word

109

has depth, significance, or none at all. For most of us words have very little depth, they have lost their weight. A river is not a particular river. The rivers of America or England or Europe or India are all rivers. but the moment there is identification through a word, there is division. And this division is an abstraction of the river, the quality of water, the depth of the water, the volume, the flow, the beauty of the river.

IT IS DAWN in these northern latitudes. In these latitudes dawn begins very early and lasts a long time. It is one of the most beautiful things on earth, the beginning of a dawn and the beginning of a day.

After a stormy night, the trees battered about, the leaves shaken and dry branches broken, the long pursuing winds have cleansed the air, which is dry. The dawn was so slowly creeping over the earth; it had an extraordinary quality this morning, especially this morning — it is probably after the winds of yesterday. But this dawn on this particular day was something more than the dawn of other days. It was so utterly quiet. You hardly dared to breathe for fear of disturbing anything. The leaves were still, even the most tender leaves. It was as though the whole earth were holding its breath, probably in great adoration. And slowly the sun touched the top of the mountains, orange, yellow, and there were specks of light on other hills. And still there was great silence. Then the noises began — the song of birds, the red-tailed hawk hovering in the sky, and the dove began its mourning song — but the silence of the dawn was in the morning, in the whole earth.

If you walk down below the hill, high across the valley, past the orange groves and some green lawns, past the tall slender eucalyptus, you come to a hill on which there are many buildings. It is an institute for something or other, and across the valley there is a long golf course, beautifully kept; we have played on it long ago. One has forgotten the course, the bunkers, but there it still is, very carefully maintained. One sees quite a lot of people with heavy bags playing on it. In the old days one had a bag of

*Krishnamurti's 88th birthday.

111

only six clubs but now there are about a dozen. It is getting too professional, too expensive.

You come over to another hill, and there too there are several institutions, foundations, organizations of almost every kind. All over the world there are dozens of institutions, forums, inner and outer directive groups. Everywhere you go in the so-called free world there is every kind of institution, organization, forum, to do this and to do that, to bring peace to man, to preserve the wilderness, to save the various animals and so on. It is quite bewildering and quite common now — groups of this and groups of that, each group with its own leaders, its own presidents and secretaries, the man who started it and the others who followed him. It is quite extraordinary, all these little organizations and institutions. And slowly they begin to deteriorate; probably it is inherent in all institutions, including the institutions that help man outwardly, like the institutions for greater knowledge. Those are probably necessary, but one is rather startled that there are also these inner directed groups of various types which do different kinds of meditation. They are rather curious those two words 'inner directed' — who is the director and what is the direction? Is the director different from the direction? We never seem to ask fundamental questions.

There are organizations to help man in the physical world, controlled by men who in themselves have their problems and their ambitions and achievements, worshipping success, but that seems to be almost inevitable and that kind of thing has been going on for thousands and thousands of years. But are there institutions to study man or bring peace to man? Do various systems, based on some conclusion, actually help man? Apparently all the organizers in the world feel they do, but have they actually helped man to be free from his sorrow, pain, anxiety and all the travail of life? Can an outside agency, however exalted, however established in some kind of mystical ideational tradition, in any way change man?

What will fundamentally bring about a radical change in man's brutality, end the wars he has been through and the constant conflict in which he lives? Will knowledge help him? If you like to use that word, evolution — man has evolved through knowledge. From ancient days he has gathered a great deal of information, knowledge about the world around him, above him, from the bullock cart to the jet, from the jet to going to the moon, and so on. There is tremendous advancement in all this. But has this knowledge in any way put an end to his selfishness, to his aggressive, competitive recklessness? Knowledge, after all, is to be aware of and to know all the things of the world, how the world was created, the achievements of man from the beginning to the present day. We are all well informed, some more, some less, but inwardly we are very primitive, almost barbarous, however cultured we may be outwardly, however well informed about many, many things, able to argue, to convince, to come to some decisions and conclusions. This can go on endlessly outwardly. There are dozens and dozens of specialists of every kind, but one asks seriously: can any kind of outside agency, including god, help man to end his grief, his utter loneliness, confusion, anxiety and so on? Or must he always live with that, put up with it, get used to it and say that it is part of life? The vast majority of mankind throughout the world tolerate it, accept it. Or they have institutions to pray to something outside — pray for peace, hold demonstrations for peace, but there is no peace in the heart of man.

What will change man? He has suffered endlessly, caught in the network of fear, ever pursuing pleasure. This has been the course of his life, and nothing seems to change it. Instead of being cynical about it all, or bitter, or angry, it is like that, life *is* that, and we ask, how can all that be changed? Certainly not by an outside agency. Man has to face it, not avoid it, and examine it without asking for any aid; he is master of himself. He has made this society, he is responsible for it, and this very responsibility demands that he bring about a change in himself. But very few pay attention to all this. For the vast mass of people, their thinking is so utterly indifferent, irresponsible, seeking to fulfil their own selfish life, sublimating their desires but still remaining selfish.

To look at all this is not being a pessimist or trying to be an optimist. One has to look at all this. And you are the only one who can change yourself and the society in which you live. That is a fact, and you can't escape from it. If you do escape from it then you are never going to have peace on this earth, never an abiding sense of joy, a sense of bliss.

The dawn is over and a new day has begun. It is really a new day, a new morning. And when one looks around, one wonders at the beauty of the land and the trees and the richness of it. It is really a new day and the wonder of it is, it is there.

BROCKWOOD PARK,* HAMPSHIRE

Monday, May 30, 1983

IT HAS BEEN raining here for over a month every day. When you come from a climate like California where the rains stopped over a month ago, where the green fields were drying up and turning brown and the sun was very hot (it was over 90° and would get hotter still, though they say it is going to be a mild summer) — when you come from that climate it is rather startling and surprising to see the green grass, the marvellous green trees and the copper beeches, which are a spreading, light brown, becoming gradually darker and darker. To see them now among the green trees is a delight. They are going to be very dark as the summer comes on. And this earth is very beautiful. Earth, whether it is desert or filled with orchards and green, bright fields, is always beautiful.

To go for a walk in the fields with the cattle and the young lambs, and in the woods with the song of birds, without a single thought in your mind, only watching the earth, the trees, the sheep and hearing the cuckoo calling and the wood pigeons; to walk without any emotion, any sentiment, to watch the trees and all the earth: when you so watch, you learn your own thinking, are aware of your own reactions and do not allow a single thought to escape you without understanding why it came, what was the cause of it. If you are watchful, never letting a thought go by, then the brain becomes very quiet. Then you watch in great silence and that silence has immense depth, a lasting incorruptible beauty.

The boy was good at games, really quite good. He was also

---

*From May 14–22 there was a gathering at Ojai during which Krishnamurti gave four talks and held Question and Answer meetings. On May 27 he flew to England and went to stay at his school at Brockwood Park.

good at his studies; he was serious. So one day he came to his teacher and said, 'Sir, could I have a talk with you?' The educator said, 'Yes, we can have a talk; let us go out for a walk.' So they had a dialogue. It was a conversation between the teacher and the taught, a conversation in which there was some respect on both sides, and as the educator was also serious, the conversation was pleasant, friendly, and they had forgotten that he was a teacher with a student; the rank was forgotten, the importance of one who knows, the authority, and the other who is curious.

'Sir, I wonder if you know what all this is about, why I am getting an education, what part will it play when I grow up, what role have I in this world, why do I have to study, why do I have to marry and what is my future? Of course I realize I have to study and pass some sort of exams and I hope I will be able to pass them. I will probably live for some years, perhaps fifty, sixty or more, and in all those years to come what will be my life and the life of those people around me? What am I going to be and what is the point of these long hours over books and hearing the teachers? There might be a devastating war; we might all be killed. If death is all that lies ahead, then what is the point of all this education? Please, I am asking these questions quite seriously because I have heard the other teachers and you too pointing out many of these things.'

'I would like to take one question at a time. You have asked many questions, you have put several problems before me, so first let us look at perhaps the most important question: what is the future of mankind and of yourself? As you know, your parents are fairly well off and of course they want to help you in any way they can. Perhaps if you get married they might give you a house, buy a house with all the things necessary in it, and you might have a nice wife — might. So what is it you are going to be? The usual mediocre person? Get a job, settle down with all the problems around you and in you — is that your future? Of course a war may come, but it may not happen; let us hope it does not happen. Let us hope man may come to realize that wars of any kind will never solve any human problem. Men may improve, they may invent better aeroplanes and so on but wars have never solved human problems and they never will. So let us forget for the moment that all of us might be destroyed through the craziness of super powers, through the craziness of terrorists or some demagogue in some country wanting to destroy his invented enemies. Let us forget all that for the moment. Let us consider what is your future, knowing that you are part of the rest of the world. What is your future? As I asked, to be a mediocre person? Mediocrity means to go half way up the hill, half way in anything, never going to the very top of the mountain or demanding all your energy, your capacity, never demanding excellence.

'Of course you must realize also that there will be all the pressures from outside — pressures to do this, all the various narrow religious sectarian pressures and propaganda. Propaganda can never tell the truth; truth can never be propagated. So I hope you realize the pressure on you — pressure from your parents, from your society, from the tradition to be a scientist, to be a philosopher, to be a physicist, a man who undertakes research in any field; or to be a business man. Realizing all this, which you must do at your age, what way will you go? We have been talking about all these things for many terms, and probably, if one may point out, you have applied your mind to all this. So as we have some time together to go around the hill and come back, I am asking you, not as a teacher but with affection as a friend genuinely concerned, what is your future? Even if you have already made up your mind to pass some exams and have a career, a good profession, you still have to ask, is that all? Even if you do have a good profession, perhaps a life that is fairly pleasant, you will have a lot of troubles, problems. If you have a family, what will be the future of your children? This is a question that you have to answer yourself and perhaps we can talk about it. You have to consider the future of your children, not just your own future, and you have to consider the future of humanity, forgetting that you are German, French, English or Indian. Let us talk about it, but please realize I am not telling you what you should do. Only fools advise, so I am not entering into that category. I am just questioning in a friendly manner, which I hope you realize; I am not pushing you, directing you, persuading you. What is your future? Will you mature rapidly or slowly, gracefully, sensitively? Will you be mediocre, though you may be first class in your profession? You may excel, you may be very, very good at whatever you do, but I am talking of mediocrity of the mind, of the heart, mediocrity of your entire being.'

'Sir, I don't really know how to answer these questions. I have not given too much thought to it, but when you ask this question, whether I am to become like the rest of the world, mediocre, I certainly don't want to be that. I also realize the attraction of the world. I also see that part of me wants all that. I want to have some fun, some happy times, but the other side of me also sees the danger of all that, the difficulties, the urges, the temptations. So I really don't know where I will end up. And also, as you pointed out on several occasions, I don't know myself what I am. One thing is definite, I really don't want to be a mediocre person with a small mind and heart, though with a brain that may be extraordinarily clever. I may study books and acquire a great deal of knowledge, but I may still be a very limited, narrow person. Mediocrity, sir, is a very good word which you have used and when I look at it I am getting frightened — not of the word but of the whole implications of what you have shown. I really don't know, and perhaps in talking it over with you it may clear things up. I can't so easily talk with my parents. They probably have had the same problems as I have; they may be more mature physically but they may be in the same position as I am. So if I may ask, sir, may I take another occasion, if you are willing, to talk with you? I really feel rather frightened, nervous, apprehensive of my capacity to meet all this, face it, go through it and not become a mediocre person.'

It was one of those mornings that has never been before: the near meadow, the still beeches and the lane that goes into the deeper wood — all was silence. There wasn't a bird chirping and the nearby horses were standing still. A morning like this, fresh, tender, is a rare thing. There is peace in this part of the land and everything was very quiet. There was that feeling, that sense of absolute silence. It was not a romantic sentimentalism, not poetic imagination. It was and is. A simple thing is all this is. The copper beeches this morning were full of splendour against the green fields stretching to the distance, and a cloud full of that morning light was floating lazily by. The sun was just coming up, there was great peace and a sense of adoration. Not the adoration of some god or imaginative deity but a reverence that is born of great beauty. This morning one could let go all the things one has gathered and be silent with the woods and the trees and the quiet lawn. The sky was a pale and tender blue and far away across the fields a cuckoo was calling, the wood pigeons were cooing and the blackbirds began their morning song. In the distance you could hear a car going by. Probably when the heavens are so quiet with loveliness it will rain later on. It always does when the early morning is very clear. But this morning it was all very special, something that has never been before and could never be again.

'I am glad you have come of your own accord, without being invited, and perhaps if you are prepared, we can continue with our conversation about mediocrity and the future of your life. One can be excellent in one's career; we aren't saying that there is mediocrity in all professions; a good carpenter may not be mediocre in his work but in his daily, inward life, his life with his family, he may be. We both understand the meaning of that word now and we should investigate together the depth of that word. We are talking about inward mediocrity, psychological conflicts, problems and travail. There can be great scientists who yet inwardly lead a mediocre life. So what is going to be your life? In some ways you are a clever student, but for what will you use your brain? We are not talking about your career, that will come later; what we should be concerned about is the way you are going to live. Of course you are not going to be a criminal in the ordinary sense of that word. You are not, if you are wise, going to be a bully; they are too aggressive. You will probably get an excellent job, do excellent work in whatever you choose to do. So let us put that aside for a moment; but inside, what is your life? Inwardly, what is the future? Are you going to be like the rest of the world, always hunting pleasure, always troubled with a dozen psychological problems?'

'At present, sir, I have no problems, except the problems of passing examinations and the weariness of all that. Otherwise I seem to have no problems. There is a certain freedom. I feel happy, young. When I see all these old people I ask myself, am I going to end up like that? They seem to have had good careers or to have done something they wanted to do but in spite of that they become dreary, dull, and they seem never to have excelled in the deeper qualities of the brain. I certainly don't want to be like that. It is not vanity but I want to have something different. It is not an ambition. I want to have a good career and all that business but I certainly in no way want to be like these old people who seem to have lost everything they like.'

'You may not want to be like them but life is a very demanding and cruel thing. It won't let you alone. You will have great pressure from society whether you live here or in America or in any other part of the world. You will be constantly urged to become like the rest, to become something of a hypocrite, say things you don't really mean, and if you do marry that may raise problems too. You must understand that life is a very complex affair — not just pursuing what you want to do and being pig-headed about it. These young people want to become something — lawyers, engineers, politicians and so on; there is the urge, drive of ambition for power, money. That is what those old people whom you talk about have been through. They are worn out by constant conflict, by their desires. Look at it, look at the people around you. They are all in the same boat. Some leave the boat and wander endlessly and die. Some seek some peaceful corner of the earth and retire; some join a monastery, become monks of various kinds, taking desperate vows. The vast majority, millions and millions, lead a very small life, their horizon is very limited. They have their sorrows, their joys and they seem never to escape from them or understand them and go beyond. So again we ask each other, what is our future, specifically what is your future? Of course you are much too young to go into this question very deeply, for youth has nothing to do with the total comprehension of this question. You may be an agnostic; the young do not believe in anything, but as you grow older then you turn to some form of religious superstition, religious dogma, religious conviction. Religion is not an opiate, but man has made religion in his own image, blind comfort and therefore security. He has made religion into something totally unintelligent and impracticable, not something that you can live with. How old are you?'

'I'm going to be nineteen, sir. My grandmother has left me something when I am twenty-one and perhaps before I go to the university I can travel and look around. But I will always carry this question with me wherever I am, whatever my future. I may marry, probably I will, and have children, and so the great question arises — what is their future? I am somewhat aware of what the politicians are doing right throughout the world. It is an ugly business as far as I am concerned, so I think I won't be a politician. I'm pretty sure of that but I want a good job. I'd like to work with my hands and with my brain but the question will be how not to become a mediocre person like ninety-nine per cent of the world. So, sir, what am I to do? Oh, yes I am aware of churches and temples and all that; I am not attracted to them. I rather revolt against all that — the priests and the hierarchy of authority, but how am I going to prevent myself becoming an ordinary, average, mediocre person?'

'If I may suggest, never under any circumstances ask "how". When you use the word "how" you really want someone to tell you what to do, some guide, some system, somebody to lead you by the hand so that you lose your freedom, your capacity to observe, your own activities, your own thoughts, your own way of life. When you ask "how" you really become a second-hand human being; you lose integrity and also the innate honesty to look at yourself, to be what you are and to go beyond and above what you are. Never, never ask the question "how". We are talking psychologically, of course. You have to ask "how" when you want to put a motor together or build a computer. You have to learn something about it from somebody. But to be psychologically free and original can only come about when you are aware of your own inward activities, watch what you are thinking and never let one thought escape without observing the nature of it, the source of it. Observing, watching. One learns about oneself much more by watching than from books or from some psychologist or complicated, clever, erudite scholar or professor.

'It is going to be very difficult, my friend. It can tear you in many directions. There are a great many so-called temptations —biological, social, and you can be torn apart by the cruelty of society. Of course you are going to have to stand alone but that can come about not through force, determination or desire but when you begin to see the false things around you and in yourself: the emotions, the hopes. When you begin to see that which is false, then there is the beginning of awareness, of

122

intelligence. You have to be a light to yourself and it is one of the most difficult things in life.'

'Sir, you have made it all seem so very difficult, so very complex, so very awesome, frightening.'

'I am just pointing all this out to you. It doesn't mean that facts need frighten you. Facts are there to observe. If you observe them they never frighten you. Facts are not frightening. But if you want to avoid them, turn your back and run, then that is frightening. To stand, to see that what you have done may not have been totally correct, to live with the fact and not interpret the fact according to your pleasure or form of reaction, that is not frightening. Life isn't very simple. One can live simply but life itself is vast, complex. It extends from horizon to horizon. You can live with few clothes or with one meal a day, but that is not simplicity. So be simple, don't live in a complicated way, contradictory and so on, just be simple inwardly. . . . You played tennis this morning. I was watching and you seem to be quite good at it. Perhaps we will meet again. That is up to you.'

'Thank you, sir.'

Ojai,* California

Tuesday, March 27, 1984

ON THAT DRIVE from the airport through the vulgarity of large towns spreading out for many, many miles, with glaring lights and so much noise, then taking the freeway and going through a small tunnel, you suddenly came upon the Pacific. It was a clear day without a breath of wind but as it was early morning there was a freshness before the pollution of the monoxide gas filled the air. The sea was so calm, almost like an immense lake. And the sun was just coming over the hill, and the deep waters of the Pacific were the colour of the Nile, but at the edges they were light blue, gently lapping the shores. And there were many birds and you saw in the distance a whale.

Following the coast road, there were very few cars that morning, but houses everywhere; probably very rich people lived there. And you saw the the pleasant hills on the left when you arrived at the Pacific. There were houses right up among the hills and the road wound in and out, following the sea, and again came upon another town, but fortunately the highway didn't go through it.

There was a naval centre there with its modern means of killing humanity. And you went along and turned to the right, leaving the sea behind, and after the oil wells, you drove further away from the sea, through orange groves, past a golf course, to a small village, the road winding through orange orchards, and the air was filled with the perfume of orange blossom. And all the

*On June 6, 1983, Dorothy Simmons, the Principal of Brockwood Park School, had a heart attack. Thereafter Krishnamurti was too busy with school affairs for any more dictations. On July 1 he went to Saanen, Switzerland, for the international annual gathering. On August 15 he returned to Brockwood for a gathering there, and on October 22 he flew to Delhi. He did not get back to Ojai until February 22, 1984. Unfortunately he dictated only three more pieces.

124

leaves of the trees were shining. There seemed to be such peace in this valley, so quiet, away from all crowds and noise and vulgarity. This country is beautiful, so vast — with deserts, snow-capped mountains, villages, great towns and still greater rivers. The land is marvellously beautiful, vast, all inclusive.

And we came to this house which was still more quiet and beautiful, recently built and with the cleanliness that houses in towns don't have. There were lots of flowers, roses and so on. A place in which to be quiet, not just vegetate, but to be really deeply, inwardly, quiet. Silence is a great benediction, it cleanses the brain, gives vitality to it, and this silence builds up great energy, not the energy of thought or the energy of machines but that unpolluted energy, untouched by thought. It is the energy that has incalculable capacity, skills. And this is a place where the brain, being very active, can be silent. That very intense activity of the brain has the quality and the depth and the beauty of silence.

Though one has repeated this often, education is the cultivation of the whole brain, not one part of it; it is a holistic cultivation of the human being. A High school or Secondary school should teach both science and religion. Science really means the cultivation of knowledge, doesn't it? Science is what has brought about the present state of tension in the world for it has put together through knowledge the most destructive instrument that man has ever found. It can wipe out whole cities at one blow, millions can be destroyed in a second. A million human beings can be vaporized. And science has also given us a great many beneficial things — communication, medicine, surgery and innumerable small things for the comfort of man, for an easy way of life in which human beings need not struggle endlessly to gather food, cook and so on. And it has given us the modern deity, the computer. One can enumerate the many, many things that science has brought about to help man and also to destroy man, destroy the entire world of humanity and the vast beauty of nature. Governments are using the scientists, and scientists like to be used by governments for then they have a position, money, recognition and so on. Human beings also look to science to bring about peace in the world, but it has failed, just as politics and the politicians have failed to give them total security, peace to live and cultivate not only the fields but their brain, their heart, their way of living, which is the highest art.

And religions — the accepted, traditional, superficial religions, creeds and dogmas — have brought about great damage in the world. They have been responsible for wars in history dividing man against man — one whole continent with very strong beliefs, rituals, dogmas against another continent which does not believe the same things, does not have the same symbols, the same rituals. This is not religion, it is just repetition of a tradition, of endless rituals that have lost meaning except that they give some kind of stimulus; it has become a vast entertainment. Religion is something entirely different. We have often spoken about religion. The essence of religion is freedom, not to do what you like, that is too childish, too immature and too contradictory, bringing great conflict, misery and confusion. Freedom again is something entirely different. Freedom means to have no conflict, psychologically, inwardly. And with freedom the brain becomes holistic, not fragmented in itself. Freedom also means love, compassion, and there is no freedom if there is not intelligence. Intelligence is inherent in compassion and love. We can go into this endlessly, not verbally or intellectually, but inwardly live a life of such a nature.

And in a Secondary school or a High school, science is knowledge. Knowledge can expand endlessly, but that knowledge is always limited because knowledge is based on experience and that experience may be a theoretical, hypothetical result. Knowledge is necessary but as long as science is the activity of a separate group, or a separate nation, which is tribal activity, such knowledge can only bring about greater conflict, greater havoc in the world, which is what is happening now.

Science with its knowledge is not for destroying human beings because scientists after all are human beings first, not just specialists; they are ambitious, greedy, seeking their own personal security like all the other human beings in the world. They are like you and another. But their specialization is bringing great destruction as well as some benefit. The last two great wars have shown this. Humanity seems to be in a perpetual movement of destruction and building up again — destroy and build; destroy human beings and give birth to a greater population. But if all the scientists in the world put their tools down and said, 'We will not contribute to war, to destroying humanity', they could turn their attention, their skill, their commitment to bringing about a better relationship between nature, environment and human beings.

If there is some peace among a few people, then those few, not necessarily the élite, will employ all their skill to bring about a different world, then religion and science can go together.

Religion is a form of science. That is, to know and to go beyond all knowledge, to comprehend the nature and immensity of the universe, not through a telescope, but the immensity of the mind and the heart. And this immensity has nothing whatsoever to do with any organized religion. How easily man becomes a tool of his own belief, his own fanaticism, committed to some kind of dogma which has no reality. No temple, no mosque, no church, holds truth. They are symbols perhaps but symbols are not the actual. In worshipping a symbol you will lose the real, the truth. But unfortunately the symbol has been given far greater importance than truth. One worships the symbol. All religions are based on some conclusions and beliefs, and all beliefs are divisive, whether political beliefs or religious.

Where there is division there must be conflict. And a High school is not a place for conflict. It is a place for learning the art of living. This art is the greatest, it surpasses all other arts, for this art touches the entire human being, not one part of him, however pleasant that may be. And in a school of this kind, if the educator is committed to this, not as an ideal, but as an actuality of daily life — committed, let's repeat again, not to some ideal, some Utopia, some noble conclusion, he can actually try to find out in the human brain a way of living that is not caught in problems, strife, conflict and pain. Love is not a movement of pain, anxiety, loneliness; it is timeless. And the educator, if he would stick at it, could instil in the students' acquisition of knowledge this true religious spirit which goes far beyond all knowledge, which is perhaps the very end of knowledge — not perhaps — it *is* the end of knowledge. For there must be freedom from knowledge to understand that which is eternal, which is timeless. Knowledge is of time, and religion is free from the bondage of time.

It seems so urgent and important that we bring about a new generation, even half a dozen people in the world would make a vast difference. But the educator needs education. It is the greatest vocation in the world.

THE PACIFIC DOES not seem to have great tides, at least not on this side of the Pacific along the coast of California. It is a very small tide, it goes in and goes out, unlike those vast tides that go out several hundred yards and come rushing in. There is quite a different sound when the tide is going out, when the flow of water is withdrawing, from when it is coming in with a certain sense of fury, a quality of sound totally different from the sound of the wind among the leaves.

Everything seems to have a sound. That tree in the field, in its solitude, has that peculiar sound of being separate from all other trees. The great sequoias have their own deep lasting ancient sound. Silence has its own peculiar sound. And of course the endless daily chatter of human beings about their business, their politics and their technological advancements and so on, has its own sound. A really good book has its peculiar vibrations of sound. The vast emptiness also has its throbbing sound.

The ebb and flow of the tide is like human action and reaction. Our actions and reactions are so quick. There isn't a pause before the reaction takes place. A question is put and immediately, instantly, one tries to seek an answer, a solution to a problem. There is not a pause between the question and the answer. After all, we are the ebb and flow of life — the outward and the inward. We try to establish a relationship with the outward, thinking that the inward is something separate, something that is unconnected with the outer. But surely the movement of the outer is the flow of the inward. They are both the same, like the waters of the sea, this constant restless movement of the outer and the inner, the response to the challenge. This is our life. When we first put together from the inward, then the inner becomes the slave of the outer. The society we have created is the outer, then to that society the inner becomes the slave. And the revolt against the outer is the same as the revolt of the inner. This constant ebb and flow, restless, anxious, fearful: can this movement ever stop? Of course the ebb and flow of the waters of the sea are entirely free from this ebb and flow of the outer and the inner — the inner becoming the outer, then the outer trying to control the inner because the external has become all important; then the reaction to that importance from the inner. This has been the way of life, a life of constant pain and pleasure.

We never seem to learn about this movement, that it is one movement. The outer and the inner are not two separate movements. The waters of the sea withdraw from the shore, then the same water comes in, lashing the shores, the cliffs. Because we have separated the external and the inner, contradiction begins, the contradiction that breeds conflict and pain. This division between the outer and the inner is so unreal, so illusory, but we keep the external totally separate from the inner. Perhaps this may be one of the major causes of conflict, yet we never seem to learn — learn not memorize, learn, which is a form of movement all the time — learn to live without this contradiction. The outer and the inner are one, a unitary movement, not separate, but whole. One may perhaps intellectually comprehend it, accept it as a theoretical statement or intellectual concept, but when one lives with concepts one never learns. The concepts become static. You may change them but the very transformation of one concept to another is still static, is still fixed. But to feel, to have the sensitivity of seeing that life is not a movement of two separate activities, the external and the inward, to see that it is one, to realize that the inter-relationship is this movement, is this ebb and flow of sorrow and pleasure, joy and depression, loneliness and the escape, to perceive non-verbally this life as a whole, not fragmented, not broken up, is to learn. Learning about it is not a matter of time, though, not a gradual process, for then time again becomes divisive. Time acts

130

in the fragmentation of the whole. But to see the truth of it in an instant, then it is there, this action and reaction, endlessly — this light and dark, the beauty and ugliness.

That which is whole is free from the ebb and flow of life, of action and reaction. Beauty has no opposite. Hate is not the opposite of love.

WALKING DOWN THE straight road on a lovely morning, it was spring, and the sky was extraordinarily blue; there wasn't a cloud in it, and the sun was just warm, not too hot. It felt nice. And the leaves were shining and a sparkle was in the air. It was really a most extraordinarily beautiful morning. The high mountain was there, impenetrable, and the hills below were green and lovely. And as you walked along quietly, without much thought, you saw a dead leaf, yellow and bright red, a leaf from the autumn. How beautiful that leaf was, so simple in its death, so lively, full of the beauty and vitality of the whole tree and the summer. Strange that it had not withered. Looking at it more closely, one saw all the veins and the stem and the shape of that leaf. That leaf was all the tree.

Why do human beings die so miserably, so unhappily, with a disease, old age, senility, the body shrunk, ugly? Why can't they die naturally and as beautifully as this leaf? What is wrong with us? In spite of all the doctors, medicines and hospitals, operations and all the agony of life, and the pleasures too, we don't seem able to die with dignity, simplicity, and with a smile.

Once, walking along a lane, one heard behind one a chant, melodious, rhythmic, with the ancient strength of Sanskrit. One stopped and looked round. An eldest son, naked to his waist, was carrying a terracotta pot with a fire burning in it. He was holding it in another vessel and behind him were two men carrying his dead father, covered with a white cloth, and they were all chanting. One knew what that chant was, one almost joined in. They went past and one followed them. They were going down the road chanting, and the eldest son was in tears. They carried

132

the father to the beach where they had already collected a great pile of wood and they laid the body on top of that heap of wood and set it on fire. It was all so natural, so extraordinarily simple: there were no flowers, there was no hearse, there were no black carriages with black horses. It was all very quiet and utterly dignified. And one looked at that leaf, and a thousand leaves of the tree. The winter brought that leaf from its mother on to that path and it would presently dry out completely and wither, be gone, carried away by the winds and lost.

As you teach children mathematics, writing, reading and all the business of acquiring knowledge, they should also be taught the great dignity of death, not as a morbid, unhappy thing that one has to face eventually, but as something of daily life — the daily life of looking at the blue sky and the grasshopper on a leaf. It is part of learning, as you grow teeth and have all the discomfort of childish illnesses. Children have extraordinary curiosity. If you see the nature of death, you don't explain that everything dies, dust to dust and so on, but without any fear you explain it to them gently and make them feel that the living and the dying are one — not at the end of one's life after fifty, sixty or ninety years, but that death is like that leaf. Look at the old men and women, how decrepit, how lost, how unhappy and how ugly they look. Is it because they have not really understood either the living or the dying? They have used life, they waste away their life with incessant conflict which only exercises and gives strength to the self, the 'me', the ego. We spend our days in such varieties of conflict and unhappiness, with some joy and pleasure, drinking, smoking, late nights and work, work, work. And at the end of one's life one faces that thing called death and is frightened of it. One thinks it can always be understood, felt deeply. The child with his curiosity can be helped to understand that death is not merely the wasting of the body through disease, old age and some unexpected accident, but that the ending of every day is also the ending of oneself every day.

There is no resurrection, that is superstition, a dogmatic

133

belief. Everything on earth, on this beautiful earth, lives, dies, comes into being and withers away. To grasp this whole movement of life requires intelligence, not the intelligence of thought, or books, or knowledge, but the intelligence of love and compassion with its sensitivity. One is very certain that if the educator understands the significance of death and the dignity of it, the extraordinary simplicity of dying — understands it not intellectually but deeply — then he may be able to convey to the student, to the child, that dying, the ending, is not to be avoided, is not something to be frightened of, for it is part of one's whole life, so that as the student, the child, grows up he will never be frightened of the ending. If all the human beings who have lived before us, past generations upon generations, still lived on this earth how terrible it would be. The beginning is not the ending.

And one would like to help — no, that's the wrong word — one would like in education to bring death into some kind of reality, actuality, not of someone else dying but of each one of us, however old or young, having inevitably to face that thing. It is not a sad affair of tears, of loneliness, of separation. We kill so easily, not only the animals for one's food but the vast unnecessary killing for amusement, called sport — killing a deer because that is the season. Killing a deer is like killing your neighbour. You kill animals because you have lost touch with nature, with all the living things on this earth. You kill in wars for so many romantic, nationalistic, political, ideologies. In the name of God you have killed people. Violence and killing go together.

As one looked at that dead leaf with all its beauty and colour, maybe one would very deeply comprehend, be aware of, what one's own death must be, not at the very end but at the very beginning. Death isn't some horrific thing, something to be avoided, something to be postponed, but rather something to be with day in and day out. And out of that comes an extraordinary sense of immensity.